Starting And Running A Do-It-Yourself Dogwash

by Doug Gelbert
owner-operator of the Dogomat Do-It-Yourself Dog Wash

STARTING AND RUNNING A DO-IT-YOURSELF DOG WASH

Cruden Bay Books
P.O. Box 467
Montchanin DE 19710

Manufactured in the United States of America

By way of introduction...

When I first started in the self-service dog wash business there was no resource like this manual available. I had first gotten the idea for such a service in 1993 after reading a two-line filler article in the *Philadelphia Inquirer* that mentioned the existence of a place in California where people paid to wash their own dogs. That was all. After doing as much research as I could into the world of self-service dog washes I still didn't know much more than I had learned in those two little lines in the newspaper. Lewis and Clark knew more about the uncharted West before embarking on the Voyage of Discovery than I knew about the do-it-yourself dog wash business before plunging in.

Hopefully that will not be the case for you.

What information I could find came from a few webpages and widely scattered articles across the country. As I was soon to learn, much of this information was highly suspect, provided as it was by people in the business whose mission was to obviously bathe themselves in the most favorable light possible. My favorite self-serving article came in the cover story of a leading pet industry trade journal. A pet store owner was raving about the tremendous success of the recent installation of a 4-station, self-service bathing area in the store. More than 300 dogs were bathed during the Grand Opening weekend alone, the owner boasted proudly. A neophyte to the dog washing business might very well read that and by doing some quick math, multiplying that number of dogs by, say $10, and conclude there was $3000 to be made in a single weekend and well over $100,000 in annual revenue from those four little tubs!

Actually being in the dog wash business it is possible to see past that propaganda. Assuming a verrrrrrrrry long weekend of 12 hours on Saturday and 8 hours on Sunday, the store would be able to achieve that level of business by averaging 15 dogs per hour - or 4 dogs per tub per hour, every hour. That gives each customer 15 minutes to wash and dry a dog (I won't even include the time required to clean each tub between 300 washes). I know most customers take at least 30 minutes to get the job done, hardly any are in and out in 15 minutes. But giving the store owner the benefit of the doubt and assuming his customers were all herded out in 15 minutes, he would still need divine intervention to get exactly 4 customers to show up every 15 minutes to keep the assembly line humming. Anyone in the dog wash business knows that most of those 300 people are going to want to wash a dog between 10 a.m. and 2 p.m. on Saturday.

The moral of the story is that no matter how much people tell you about their business and how much you study you are never really going to know what a business is like until you jump in yourself. That is the mission of this manual - to walk you to the edge of the diving board with as much knowledge as I have gathered in more than 5 years of the self-service dog wash business. But I don't know what the waters will be like when you jump in. You may do fabulously well in the self-service dog wash business, better than I could ever imagine, or you may be do miserably. How anyone else has done in the business before you is largely irrelevant. It is your journey that matters. You are reading this book because the flicker of entrepreneurial spirit glows inside you. The information that follows will only fan that exciting flame.

Safe rails,
Doug

Starting And Running A Do-It-Yourself Dog Wash
Section One: Starting and Operating

Starting and And Running A Do-It-Yourself Dogwash

Section One:
Starting and Operating

The Dog Wash Concept

IS THIS A NEW IDEA?

Dog washes began appearing in southern California in the early 1980s and gained gradual acceptance among pet owners. By late 1993, however, *Pet Product News* was reporting that, "self-service dog wash shops are increasingly becoming a popular and profitable venture within the pet industry."

While some dog wash shops operate as stand-alone businesses, many are part of an existing pet store's line of services. An occasional grooming shop has added a tub or two for self-service bathing. Some dog wash shops even sport a coffee bar where owners can relax after a bath.

HOW DOES IT BENEFIT THE DOG FOR THE OWNER TO USE A DO-IT-YOURSELF DOG WASH?

◆ Reduces stress to be washed and ministered to by the owner since pets, like small children, can be traumatized by being handled by strangers;
◆ Reduces stress since some groomers use tranquilizers;
◆ Reduces stress since some dogs are not accustomed to being confined to a crate, as they must be at a groomer;
◆ Reduces stress to geriatric and infirm dogs to be attended to by the owner.

And of course, a visit to the dog wash is fun for owner and dog!

CAN A DOG WASH BE SUCCESSFUL ANYWHERE?

Today, you will find dog washes not only in sunny, snowless California but in the Rocky Mountains and the upper Midwest as well. It seems that wherever dogs are getting dirty you can operate a dog wash.

IS THERE ANYWHERE I CAN RESEARCH THE SELF-SERVICE DOG WASH BUSINESS?

Unfortunately, there is no trade association for self-service dogwashes and no industry information available. The only place to learn about running a dog wash is from dog wash owners. That is why we produced this manual.

Determining Your Market

HOW DO I DEFINE MY TRADING AREA?

Most of your customers will drive from 20 to 30 minutes to get to your shop; some will come from as far as 45 minutes away. To facilitate the management of your promotion you should divide your trading area into three segments:

- ◆ "A" Market - those customers who can reach your shop in less than 20 minutes
- ◆ "B" Market - the customers that can reach you in 20-40 minutes
- ◆ "C" Market - those customers that must drive more than 40 minutes to reach your shop

Clearly, you will concentrate your promotional efforts on your "A" market. Unless you are establishing your dog wash business in an unfamiliar community, you will already have a good feel for your trading area before you set up shop.

HOW DO I DETERMINE HOW MANY DOGS ARE IN MY TRADING AREA?

There is no dog census in the United States. One way you can estimate your potential market size is to check the number of dog licenses in your town or county, but this will be a low estimate. Half of the people in Philadelphia, for instance, do not license their automobiles - how many are going to license a dog?

There are more than 60,000,000 dogs in the United States and 270,000,000 people, roughly one dog for every five people. Assuming the dog population is fairly consistent across the country, you can guess that there will be one dog for every five people in your community. Thus, a trading area of 100,000 people can be expected to contain 20,000 dogs.

14

HOW CAN I KNOW IF DOG OWNERS IN MY AREA WILL USE MY DOG WASH?

You can't. Yours is probably the first dog wash to be tried in your community. You are a pioneer. You can interview prospective customers, you can talk to other business owners, you can pick the brains of others in pet-related businesses in your area - but you won't know for sure until you open your doors. By all means, do talk to all these folks - and more. Ask questions, evaluate the business climate in your community, visit similar businesses. Gather as much pre-opening information as you can but ultimately only your being in business will tell you if you will have any business.

HOW CAN I FORECAST SALES?

Sales forecasting is more an art than exact science. There are no trade figures on dog washes and historical data is unobtainable. Use a three-column guesstimate with scenarios for worst case, most likely case, and best case (See Topic 26, Financial Documents). Make your estimates on the conservative side because the ramifications for a bad guess will be considerably fewer.

> *The greatest pleasure of a dog is that you may make a fool of yourself with him, and not only will he not scold you, but he will make a fool of himself, too.*
> *-Samuel Butler*

The Dog Wash Customer

WHY WOULD ANYONE PAY MONEY TO WASH THEIR DOG IN A DOG WASH?

There are always two reasons a customer will use any service: it saves time or it saves money. We have found that the most important reasons people come to a dogwash are:

1. **No clean-up at home.** Cleaning up a bathroom after a close encounter of the hairy kind with a dog can take as long as an hour to make it fit for human consumption again. That is a drain on anybody's time and not a fun chore.
2. **Ease of bathing.** The dog is restrained in front of you, not writhing at the end of a chain in the back yard. The owner is standing comfortably, in control and not breaking a back bending over a bathtub trying to tackle a wet, slippery dog.
3. **Affordability and Value.** For a dog that doesn't require special handling, the cost is a fraction of what a groomer will charge for a bath.
4. **No place to wash at home.** When home is an apartment and the shower is a stall, there are some owners who really have no facility to wash a dog at home.
5. **Saves time.** Aside from clean-up time, there is the preparation time, the extra time trying to bathe and dry a dog with inadequate equipment. If the dog is bathed by a groomer, it is a two-stop process requiring a drop-off and pick-up - and in between the two trips the dog needs to be caged.Why go through the hassle when only a quick stop at the local dog wash is required?
6. **Like to fuss with the dog themselves.** Many owners want to do routine maintenance of their dogs but don't have a grooming table or other amenities found at a dog wash. They welcome the chance to be "groomer."
7. **Bad experience at groomer.** Some pets will come home from a groomer traumatized to such an extent that the owner can no longer take the dog for professional grooming.

WHO WILL MY CUSTOMERS BE?

All sorts of dog owners will use your facility. Roughly, the demographics will be:

- ◆   Age 25-40   29%
- ◆   Age 40-55   51%
- ◆   Age 55+   20%

- ◆   Male   23%
- ◆   Female   46%
- ◆   Couples   31%

Clearly, if you had to define a target market, it would be middle-aged women. But consider the other segments as well. About one in three of your customers will be couples so a trip to the dog wash is happily a family outing for many.

The dogs you will see will mirror the most popular American breeds - labrador retrievers, rottweilers, german shepherds, and golden retrievers will be your most frequent visitors. You will also see a great many bassett hounds, which need frequent bathing. Not all of your customers will be large dogs - far from it. Between 20%-30% of your dogs will be small dogs. About 10% of your customers will bring two or more dogs.

HOW MUCH MONEY DO AMERICANS SPEND ON THEIR DOGS?

The pet industry is, according to the *New York Times* (5/28/95), "exploding." Americans spend $22 billion on their pets every year, with $2 billion spent solely on grooming. That figure is increasing 10% annually and is only going to get bigger. Currently, six in ten U.S. households has a dog or cat, with the highest penetration of pet ownership coming at ages 45-54, traditionally the time when children leave home (nearly two-thirds of dog owners say caring for their pet fulfills a need for parenting). And, millions of baby boomers will become empty nesters in the coming years as the "pig moves through the python." Further, more people than ever are living alone - another indicator of pet ownership - which will only add to the ranks of America's 63.8 million dogs.

And will any of these people be willing to spend $10 every six weeks to wash their dog? Perhaps a better question might be, how are you going to stop them? Consider:

- 91% of dog owners report talking "baby talk" to their pets and buy them holiday gifts;
- 13% call home and talk to their dogs on the answering machine;
- 21% leave a television or radio on for their dog when away;
- 13% buy a house with the dog in mind;
- Dog perfume is a stampeding $10,000,000-a-year business;
- An estimated one million dogs are named as beneficiaries in wills.

HOW MUCH IS A CUSTOMER WORTH?

As you go along with your dog wash business, you will want to determine how much it costs to acquire a new customer. To compute this value, answer these questions:

- Assuming your continued good service, how long will the average customer continue to use your dog wash?
- How many times will the average customer visit your dog wash in the course of a year and how much will he spend?
- How much does it cost for you to provide your service to each customer?

For example, let's say your average customer can be expected to wash his dog four times a year, spending an average of $12 per visit. You have every reason to believe this pattern will continue for eight years. So that new customer who walks through your door is worth $384 in revenue. It will cost you about $92 to provide your goods and services to him. Thus, a new customer is worth $292 to you.

This is important knowledge. It enables you to know how much you can afford to spend to acquire a new customer. And more importantly, it reminds you how much it will cost you to lose a valued customer.

Shop Location

WHAT IS THE RELATIONSHIP BETWEEN RENT AND ADVERTISING?

Store rents will be higher in high-traffic, high-visibility areas. But since more people will see your shop you will not have to spend as much in advertising. You may want to locate in an area with little drive-by traffic and pay less rent. But be prepared to spend more in advertising to get people to know where you are. The real cost of the space you rent will always be RENT + ADVERTISING. And advertising is always riskier than a good location.

IS IT BETTER TO BE LOCATED IN A FREE-STANDING BUILDING OR IN A STRIP SHOPPING CENTER?

We prefer a free-standing building, for several reasons. There is not as much vehicular traffic in the parking lot for the owners and dogs to contend with. There is no problem with neighbors who may not appreciate the occasional barking dog. You will probably have more doors and windows. You can build your own shop identity.

The advantages of locating in a strip center include: drawing on your neighbor's customers, it is often easier for first-timers to find you, and the possibility of cooperative promotions.

A good location makes it easy for your customers to find you and you want to give yourself every advantage by making it easy for customers to do business with you.

WHAT ARE SOME OF THE THINGS I SHOULD BE ON THE LOOKOUT FOR WHEN SCOUTING FOR A LOCATION?

Before you rent a storefront, find out why it is vacant in the first place. How long has it been empty? Try and locate the former tenant and ask why he has moved.

Be wary of unoccupied buildings for rent in the area - unless you are ready to be a retail pioneer. This is the sign of a poor business area and customers tend to shy away from areas of vacant buildings.

Once you have a site in mind, spend an entire day there. Talk to other merchants and learn as much as you can about the area and its shoppers. Evaluate if these businesses will enhance your operation. Observe the traffic flow - is it steady, does it congest at rush hour? Is there a supermarket or other large retailer nearby that will draw customers to your area?

Before you negotiate a lease, talk to the building inspector and the health inspector and find out what building codes and health codes apply to your intended dog wash.

Drive around the immediate area and observe the nearby neighborhoods. Are there mostly apartments (apartment dwellers tend to own cats)? Are there many nearby housing developments (a sign of dog owners)?

HOW IMPORTANT IS MY LOCATION TO THE IMAGE OF MY BUSINESS?

Your location will determine the image you project to the public. There may be space available in the region's upscale shopping center but will that help your business? Would you rather have a liquor store or a toy store as a neighbor? You probably will want to create a family aura around your business and your neighborhood will be a large part of that image-building.

HOW MUCH SPACE WILL I NEED?

A dog wash can be run successfully in 800 square feet and comfortably in 1000 to 1200 square feet.

Ever consider what they must think of us? I mean, here we come back from the grocery store with the most amazing haul - chicken, pork, half a cow...they must think we are the greatest hunters on earth!
-Anne Tyler

Government Regulations

WHAT LICENSES WILL I NEED TO OBTAIN FOR A SELF-SERVICE DOG WASH?

Most likely, depending on your local regulations, all you will need to obtain is a general business license. If your community has more detailed requirements, consider yourself a grooming shop and comply with all regulations for a dog grooming business.

WHAT IS A FICTITIOUS NAME STATEMENT?

When a business goes by any name other than the owner's real name, you must file a fictitious name statement with the county clerk. The name must then be published in a newspaper of "general circulation" in your trading area. This will keep anyone from using the name.

DO I NEED A FEDERAL IDENTIFICATION NUMBER?

Not unless you will be hiring employees for your shop. With a Federal Identification Number the Internal Revenue Service will automatically send quarterly and year-end payroll tax returns that you must fill out even if you have no employees. So do not apply until you become an employer. You will, however, have to obtain an FID if your form of business is a partnership or corporation, regardless of whether you have employees or not.

If you pick up a starving dog and make him prosperous, he will not bite you. This is the principal difference between a dog and a man.
-Mark Twain

WHAT KIND OF INSURANCE WILL I NEED TO OPEN A SELF-SERVICE DOG WASH?

Liability will be your biggest concern. Shop around for a "business owner's package" that covers all risks and replacement cost insurance. Many of the large companies have policies created specifically for pet groomers.

Premiums are often based on the gross revenues of the business but can also be based on the square footage in your shop. Your lease may also require that you carry certain types of insurance.

WHAT QUESTIONS SHOULD I ASK OF MY INSURANCE PROVIDER?

- ◆ What is covered and what is not?
- ◆ What are the limits of coverage and the difference in premiums?
- ◆ What pre-existing conditions are included with the policy?
- ◆ Is there a waiting period for enforcement?
- ◆ What are the cancellation conditions and notification requirements?

WHAT ABOUT GOVERNMENT INSURANCE?

Once you become an employer, Social Security (FICA) and worker's compensation are legally mandated.

*If dogs could talk it would take a lot
of the fun out of owning one.
-Andy Rooney*

Plumbing

ARE THERE ANY GOVERNMENT RESTRICTIONS AGAINST A SELF-SERVICE DOG WASH?

You will need to check with your local authorities but generally the self-service wash is treated no differently than a grooming shop. If you need to make extensive plumbing alterations to sustain your operation you will need to do so in accordance with local permits. One of your criteria in selecting a location will be whether the space will allow for the plumbing improvements you will need to make. If the water source is not convenient to where you plan to install your tubs and you still want to lease or buy the space, do not give up hope. You may be able to avoid tearing up walls and concrete floors by running the water pipes exposed alongside the inner wall. You are designing a dog wash, not a Four Seasons hotel. And some people prefer this retro "industrial" look besides.

WHAT KIND OF WATER HEATER WILL I NEED?

You will need at least a 50-gallon water heater; ideally up to 80 gallons. The most important factor in selecting a hot water heater is the recovery rate: the number of gallons of water the heater can raise 100 degrees in one hour. The amount of hot water you can draw from the heater per hour equals the recovery rate plus 70% of its storage capacity. For example, a 30-gallon heater with a 40-gallon-per-hour recovery rate delivers a maximum of 61 gallons of hot water in the first hour. Oil-fired heaters have a very rapid recovery rate; electric heaters are the slowest and gas is in between.

SHOULD I CONTROL THE TEMPERATURE OF THE WATER OR ALLOW THE CUS-TOMER TO CONTROL THE HOT AND COLD WATER AT THE BATHING STATION?

You can go either way. Some customers like to control the temperature (usually to give as much hot water as possible) and others don't want to fiddle with hot and cold water knobs - they have their hands full juggling dogs and shampoos. If you keep a constant temperature you will control your hot water bills. Most customers will be pleased with the water temperature you choose but you will never please everybody.

SHOULD I HAVE MY OWN WASHER AND DRYER?

Your life in the dog wash will be greatly simplified if you do. Otherwise you will need to take dirty towels home every night or make other arrangements for a clean supply of towels.

HOW MUCH WATER DOES IT TAKE TO WASH A DOG?

On the average, figure on 20 gallons - including your clean-up - for your cost estimates. You will also be using water for your washer and the bathroom as well.

Electricity

WILL I NEED TO DO ANY SPECIAL WIRING TO SET UP?

A self-service dog wash should not pose any special problems to an electrician. You do need to be sure you have an electrical board capable of handling your capacity if you have all your hair dryers going, the washer, the dryer, the air conditioner, your computer, your signs, etc. Note the electrical demands of all the applicances in your shop.

Look around and inspect the number of electrical outlets. Are there enough for what you plan when you open - and what you plan three years from now? You do not want to have to be running extension cords to install new equipment.

WILL I NEED ANY SPECIAL LIGHTING IN THE DOG WASH?

Hopefully you will have a pleasing supply of natural light. You will need direct overhead lighting in the bathing area, especially if you plan to maintain evening hours. Spotlighting and creative lighting can also present your retail offerings to best effect. As you design your bathing stations check for shadows which may fall across the work areas at different times during the day.

*No one appreciates the very special
genius of your conversation
as a dog does.*
-Christopher Morley

Outfitting The Shop

WHAT SHOULD A DOG WASH LOOK LIKE?

One of the best things about starting your own business is that you have total control over the face you show to the public. In general, a self-service dog wash should ideally have the following areas:

◆ **Waiting Area.** This is a place where you can greet the customers and get them acquainted with your service. In busy times, this is where customers will wait with their dogs. We provide some chairs, dog toys, free treats, and a selection of dog magazines in our waiting area. Here, too is our bulletin board with newspaper articles, testimonials and other news. An information table displays shop brochures, newsletters and other take-aways. The waiting area is also a good place to feature a few quick-selling impulse items.

◆ **Counter Area.** This is where you conduct business transactions.

◆ **Retail Area.** Between 100 to 200 square feet should be reserved for your retail stock - leashes and collars, brushes and combs, and treats.

◆ **Dog Wash Area.** The dog wash area should be designed so owners can maneuver their dogs easily through your shop and in and out of the bathing stations. Ideally, the bathing stations should be set up so the dogs can not see one another while being bathed.

◆ **Grooming Area.** This can be a separate section of the shop or can be part of the dog wash area. It consists of one or more grooming tables and tools for the do-it-yourselfer. If you also have professional grooming on the premises, it may be shared by the groomer and the public when the groomer is not working.

HOW MUCH SHOULD I SPEND TO DECORATE THE SHOP?

When setting up your shop it is best to remember that "it is easier to save a dollar than make a dollar." You should be thinking of what you want your new shop to look like long before you even find a location. In this time you can find "doggie decor" items in garage sales and flea markets and be on the make for other items you will need. Can you find an old cash register in an auction? Can you arrange to get the towels that area country clubs and hotels throw away when they are no longer fit for people but can still dry a dog?

The more you can do yourself, the less you will need to spend. Will you be doing the painting yourself? If your heart isn't locked up to a particular color scheme, talk to your local paint store about buying their reject paints at a discount.

SHOULD I DO ANYTHING SPECIAL TO THE FLOORS?

Carpeting has no place in a dog wash. It collects dog hair, retains dog odors and is not easily cleaned. So if the space you are using does not have carpet, do not install it. Keep your floors bare and keep them clean.

Setting Up The Bathing Station

WHAT TYPE OF BATHTUB SHOULD I USE?

Some dog washes take everyday bathtubs and build their own bathing stations. We prefer the standard stainless steel professional tubs. These tubs, when outfitted for serious groomers, can cost over $3000 but the low-end tubs run about $300. They stand waist-high and are easy to clean. The tubs come with a PVC-covered metal rack which enables the dog to stand above the dirty water.

These tubs and racks are strong enough for any dog that comes into your shop (we have had a Newfoundland and his owner in one of our tubs). The tubs are also impressive to your customers as they make your shop look professional.

WHAT ACCESSORIES ARE REQUIRED?

You will need to purchase a sprayhose and nozzle for each tub. The hoses are typically between five and six feet long and easily reach across any dog. Buy top-of-the-line, heavy duty sprayhoses ($125-$150) and you will not regret it. They are going to get alot of use.

The dogs will need to get into the tubs without being lifted. We use a three-platform pet step ($125) which most of the dogs navigate without difficulty.

The tubs feature two strong eye hooks from which a loop restraint can be attached. You will want one of these adjustable restraints for each bathing station as owners find them very helpful. For smaller dogs, the restraint can be removed from the eye hook and attached to the metal rack.

HOW DO I CONTROL ALL THE HAIR?

A specially designed hair trap ($60) should be attached to each of the tubs. These plastic traps prevent hair from getting into your system and clogging the drains. They unscrew easily for cleaning.

WHAT DO THE PEOPLE USE TO DRY THE DOGS?

We oufit each bathing station with two towels and a cannister-type, forced-air blowdryer. The dog can be dried right in the tub, placed on the floor or removed to the grooming table for drying. You may want to instruct your customers how best to dry the dog (pull water off with towels; place air nozzle against skin and blow out). They will appreciate the help and you will appreciate the time and energy saved in the bathing station.

To use blowdryers in your bathing stations you will need electrical outlets. These will need to be of the GFI (Ground Fault Interuptor) variety so as to prevent electrical shock in a wet area.

IS THERE ANYTHING ELSE I SHOULD HAVE IN THE BATHING STATION?

We place rubber, non-slip mats on the floors, which can become very wet when bathing a "shaker." It also helps if the owner wants to dry the dog on the floor of the bathing station.

Plastic grocery bags in which to place combed out hair are also a good idea. And for owners with more than one dog we have eye hooks screwed into the wall so a second pet can be kept with the owner in the bathing station. You can also have cages available for this purpose.

We also offer rubber aprons in each of the bathing stations for the owner. You can always tell a repeat customer - they are the ones making sure to put on the apron!

HOW MANY BATHING STATIONS SHOULD I ESTABLISH?

As many as you have the space for and can afford. You should have at least three and some established dog washes have as many as eight.

Supplying The Customer

WHAT SHAMPOOS SHOULD I HAVE ON HAND FOR MY CUSTOMERS TO USE?

In descending order of preference, your customers will want the following from your shampoos:

- Make my dog smell good!
- Get rid of his fleas
- No special problems or preferences
- A gentle shampoo for skin-sensitive dogs
- Help her stop itching

The best dog shampoos will lather up fast and rinse out completely. With this in mind, we offer these shampoos:

- **Odor Neutralizer** - Shampoo to eliminate all problem pet odors, including skunk encounters

- **Moisturizing Cherry Odor** - A moisturizing shampoo packing a wild cherry punch; there are many "fun" fragrances you can choose from

- **Flea and Tick Shampoo with Pyrethins** - Culled from chysanthemums, pyrethrins are nature's flea killers in this mild but potent shampoo

- **Standard Dog Shampoo** - One that lathers easily, rinses completely and leaves a pleasant fragrance

- **Tearless Puppy Shampoo** - A deep-cleaning shampoo still gentle enough for puppies and skin-sensitive dogs

- **Aloe & Citrus-based Shampoo** - The natural d-Limonene citrus will repel fleas and the deep-cleansing aloe will prevent drying of sensitive skin.

- **Oatmeal Shampoo** - Natural oatmeal cleans and soothes a dog's dry, irritated skin. It is nature's anti-itch remedy.

- **Tea Tree Oil Shampoo** - Formulated from tea tree oil, this natural shampoo cleans, deodorizes, detangles and repels fleas

- **Blueing Shampoo** - Excellent for removing stains from white-coated dogs but brightens all coats

- **Blackening Shampoo** - Intensifies black and dark coats while removing dirt and food stains

- **Creme Rinse** - Should be applied to dogs with fine or soft coats

WHAT ABOUT HUMAN SHAMPOOS?

Shampoos specially formulated for dogs contain a more alkaline pH than human shampoos, even the mildest of which will dry a dog's skin. Many human shampoos also are loaded with conditioners, which tend to lengthen the time it takes to dry the coat if residue remains.

HOW MANY OF MY CUSTOMERS WILL WANT TO DO THEIR OWN GROOMING?

Most are just looking to get a clean, fresh-smelling dog. Owners with long-haired and thick-coated animals will want to brush out their dogs. We provide a variety of brushes and a chart that tells owners which brush to use for each breed. We also provide a grooming table.

Only a small percentage of your customers will actually want to clip hair. For that reason we do not make clippers and shears available. Good ones are costly to purchase and maintain properly.

WHAT SHOULD A DOG OWNER KNOW ABOUT GROOMING?

Good grooming contributes to a dog's good health. The dog that is groomed regularly not only looks better but also feels better. Proper attention to these things can save the customer a veterinary bill down the line.

Puppies should be introduced to grooming as soon as possible so it is fun and not frightening but all dogs can benefit from regular grooming. Proper equipment is a MUST; the wrong type of brush can easily break the hair of a dog's coat or give the dog brush burn. We provides tip sheets on proper brushing technique (see Section III).

Brushing and combing must be done before bathing to avoid tangles and mats. The secret to proper brushing is to brush only a few hairs at a time. This is a handy check-list for brushing maintenance:

- **Non-shedding long coats:** Should be brushed regularly, several times a week
- **Coarse-haired dogs with soft, wooly undercoats:** Need care mostly in fall and spring when dog is changing into winter or summer coat and the dead coat must be stripped out
- **Fine-textured coats:** Brushed for dog's comfort
- **Short-coated dogs:** Brushed two times a week to keep skin and coat healthy

WILL MY CUSTOMERS WANT TO CLIP THEIR DOGS' TOENAILS?

Many will. This is a most disagreeble chore for most dog owners. Most owners do not how to do it safely and are afraid to try. We offer a tip sheet for first-timers. We supply a set of guillotine-style toenail clippers and styptic powder to staunch bleeding if a mistake is made. Baking powder or flour can also be used to stop a bleeding nail. Suggest to your customers who wish to clip nails to do so before bathing so that any bleeding will not stain a freshly washed coat.

If you know how to clip toenails, you can charge $3.00 and quickly and easily add revenue to the bottom line.

WHAT GROOMING TOOLS SHOULD I MAKE AVAILABLE?

Your customers will expect a selection of combs, brushes and scrubbrushes to groom the dog. These need not be top-of-the line tools but shop for the most durable ones you can find. Your shop should include:

Combs

◆	Fine-Toothed Comb -	should be of durable stainless steel; for soft, silky hair
◆	Medium-Toothed Comb -	for longer-haired dogs
◆	Rake -	used to loosen dead undercoat on dogs with heavy undercoat

Brushes

◆	Curry Comb -	used in circular motion will pull out short hair; best on short-haired dogs
◆	Hard Wire Slicker -	use on matted coats or when removing dead undercoat; good on legs and hocks
◆	Soft Wire Slicker -	best for hand-drying to leave coat straight and fluffy
◆	Pin Brush -	good for brushing non-tangled coat; will not break hair
◆	Natural Bristle Brush -	good for fine-haired dogs
◆	Glove Brushes -	those with fine wire promote natural shine on short-haired dogs
◆	Shedding Blade -	gets rid of unwanted hair easily and comfortably; turn it over and it scrapes away excess water

Scrub Brushes

◆	Low-Tech -	old-fashioned straw bristle scrub brush will work shampoos into coat
◆	High-Tech -	rubber-toothed scrubbrushes massage coat as shampoo is applied

IS THERE ANYTHING ELSE I CAN PROVIDE TO HELP MY CUSTOMERS?

Some owners will want to clean their dog's ears. Dogs with long coats can have hair growing in the ears. If it is not removed and the ear cleaned, ear canker - an infection characterized by a dark-colored discharge and a foul odor - can develop. Ear canker powder will dry the ear wax and enable the hair to be gently pulled out. After the hair is out, the ear should be cleaned with alcohol. As with nail-cutting this procedure should take place before bathing. To help your customers, have a supply of cotton swabs and cotton balls on hand.

WHAT IF A CUSTOMER WANTS TO BRING HER OWN SHAMPOO OR GROOMING TOOLS?

We have no problem with providing the facilities for customers who bring their own supplies. Do be on the lookout for chemical-based insectidal shampoos which should not be allowed in the shop unless you have a separate tub for their use.

If it is in stock, we have it.
-sign in farm supply store,
Ukiah, California

St

Th

SHOULD I SE

Groomin

know

ea

WHAT TYPES OF MERCHANDISE SHOULD I CARRY IN MY STORE?

You are not going to be able to compete with local and national pet stores on selection or price. Stick to the basics. The best-selling items are leashes and leads and a standard selection of grooming tools. You may also want to stock your store with dog toys.

WHAT IS THE BEST SALES STRATEGY TO USE?

Find a niche and your market and serve it. We feature a Canine Cafe of gourmet dog treats - most of which cannot be purchased anywhere in the area. There are more than two dozen selections and customers can even mix and match at the Doggie Salad Bar, where 18 different treats are available for 50¢ an ounce.

Dog owners spend more than 1.2 billion dollars on treats and chews alone. These snacks range from crunchy biscuits to canine cookies to shrimp alfredo sauces to animate dull, dry dog food. In order of sales, the most popular treats are:

1) Chews
2) Jerky
3) Biscuits

There are other niches you can fill as well. How about a Doggie Cosmetic Counter? Stock it with an assortment of colognes and fragrances (now a $10,000,000 a year business), nail polishes and high-fashion bandannas and collars.

LL GROOMING SUPPLIES?

g supplies are an excellent money-maker. Many of your customers will have never *n* about the grooming tools available for their dog until they use one in your shop. It is *y* to make a sale after that.

WHAT ABOUT DOG TOYS?

Be on the lookout for good buys on inexpensive, impulse toys you can stock. Your distributor should be able to alert you to these buys. They are good to have around for the holidays as well.

HOW BIG A PART OF MY OPERATION WILL THE RETAIL BUSINESS BE?

About 45% of the customers will purchase treats or supplies for their dog after the bath. The average purchase is around $3.50. You should expect 15-20% of your revenue to come after the dog wash.

For dogs with a sweet tooth, fruit is a better option than candy or human cookies. Dogs generally enjoy apples, berries and dried fruits.

Vendors

HOW CAN VENDORS SAVE ME MONEY?

Your vendors will be a major source of information on industry trends, new products, competitors, promotion and more. They will also likely be your biggest source of credit. Seek favorable terms of sale and if you need help, ask your vendor. It costs five times more to secure a new customer than to keep you and they will likely be as lenient as they can.

Make a vendor list and avoid becoming too dependent on one or two vendors. Comparison shopping and careful purchasing habits will provide all your profits as a small retailer.

WHAT ARE SOME QUESTIONS I SHOULD ASK VENDORS?

- What guarantees are there with the merchandise?
- When and how can I expect delivery?
- Can I get storage until the items are needed?
- Do you offer pre-ticketing of items?
- Are there price guarantees on reorders?
- Do I have full return privileges?
- Do you offer any promotional aids?

WHERE DO I ORDER SUPPLIES TO SET UP MY SHOP?

The main sources are pet industry trade shows and pet industry supply catalogs. Of the two, catalogs are certainly the most convenient. There are many catalog vendors serving the pet industry. Their prices on identical, or nearly identical items, vary broadly so you would be wise to order several and compare prices. Beware of minimum orders and shipping charges and be on the lookout for manufacturer close-outs and other special sales.

Some of the major Pet Supply catalog companies are:

Drs. Foster & Smith Inc.
2253 Air Park Road
P.O. Box 100
Rhinelander, WI 54501-0100
1-800-826-7206

Although geared primarily to the pet owner, the catalog features excellent product descriptions and pet care tips

The Dog's Outfitter
Humboldt Industrial Park
I Maplewood Drive
Hazleton, PA 18201-9798
1-800-367-3647

Wide selection of shampoos, grooming tools and equipment for the do-it-yourself shop

Groomer Direct
1989 Transit Way, Box 915
Brockport, NY 14420-0915
1-800-551-5048

Supplies for groomers and grooming shops only

J-B Wholesale Pet Supplies, Inc.
5 Raritan Road
Oakland, NJ 07436
1-800-526-0388

Offers informative product descriptions for its shampoo choices

Jeffers Pet Catalog
P.O. Box 100
Dothan, AL 36302-0100
1-800-533-3377

A wide selection for the consumer and shop owner

Jemar Pet Supplies
794 Biggs Highway
Rising Sun, MD 21911
1-800-458-6598

Many high-end products for the show crowd

New England Serum Company
P.O. Box 128
Topsfield, MA 01983-0228
1-800-637-3786

Popular catalog that features "rock bottom" prices on various useful products on first few pages

Pet Supply Closeouts
1445 Hilldale Avenue
Haverhill, MA 01832
1-978-372-8585

Independent distributor of pet supplies selling closeouts, surplus salvage, buybacks, backruptcies and overstocks; can sometimes find good buys on things you actually need

Phillips Feed & Pet Supply
Various Offices
1-800-451-2817 (Pennsylvania)
1-800-200-2469 (Florida)

Major wholesale distributor for products to resell to consumers

R.C. Steele
1989 Transit Way, Box 910
Brockport, NY 14420-0910
1-800-872-3773

Wholesale pet supplier; the consumer side of Groomer Direct

Ryan's Pet Supplies
1805 East McDowell Road
Phoenix, AZ 85006
1-800-525-PETS

A wide selection of low-end grooming products

That Pet Place
237 Centerville Road
Lancaster, PA 17603
1-888-842-8738

Wide-ranging pet product purveyor aiming at the consumer market

UPCO
3705 Pear Street
P.O. Box 969
St. Joseph, MO 64502

Low minimum order for pet supply catalog aimed at consumer

Trade Shows

WHAT ARE SOME OF THE BIG INDUSTRY TRADE SHOWS AND IS IT WORTH MY WHILE TO ATTEND?

By all means, if it is convenient to attend a pet industry trade show in your area you must go. A trade show is the best place to uncover new products, make deals with suppliers and learn from other professionals. One of the premier national shows is the Annual Pet Industry Christmas Trade Show in Chicago in early October. Information can be obtained from **H.H. Backer Associates**, 312-663-4040.

Other show organizers include:

Barkleigh Productions, 717-691-3388

World Wide Pet Supply Association, 818-447-2222

Pet Industry Joint Advisory Council-Canada, 514-630-7878

Pet Industry Distributors Association, 410-931-8100

Pet Industry Magazines

WHAT TRADE MAGAZINES WILL TELL ME MORE ABOUT HOW TO RUN MY BUSINESS?

There are plenty of publishers eager to keep you abreast of the fast-growing pet industry. Subscriptions to qualified professionals are free. Here are some of the pet industry trade magazines:

DOG AND KENNEL
7-L Dundas Circle
Greensboro, NC 27407
336-292-4047

PET BUSINESS
7-L Dundas Circle
Greensboro, NC 27407
336-292-4047

GROOM & BOARD
200 S. Michigan Avenue; Suite 840
Chicago, IL 60604
312-663-4040

THE PET DEALER
445 Broad Hollow Road
Melville, NY 11747
516-845-2700

GROOMER TO GROOMER
6 State Road; Suite 113
Mechanicsburg, PA 17055
717-691-3388

PET PRODUCT NEWS
P.O. Box 6050
Mission Viejo, CA 92690-6050
949-855-8822

PET AGE
200 S. Michigan Avenue; Suite 840
Chicago, IL 60604
312-663-4040

In Japan, young people believe owning a dog will better their chances of finding a mate. But since space is scarce, owning a dog is difficult. Rather, would-be-lovers rent dogs for romantic strolls. Rates: $50 a day for a poodle, $80 for a Golden Retriever.

HOW SHOULD I CHARGE FOR MY DOG WASHING SERVICE?

There are several ways you can go about pricing your service:

◆ Charge by the half-hour. You can rent out your bathing stations on a time basis for a flat fee. For example, you could charge $12 for one half-hour and $3 for each additional 10 minutes. The customer can wash as many dogs or take as much time as he is willing to pay for.

◆ Charge by the size of the dog. Some dog washes charge by the size of the dog, basing the price differential either on height or weight. For example $5 for the smallest dog up to $15 for a large dog. Of course, a small dog with a great deal of hair can require more shampoo and time than a short-coated large breed. You will also need an iron-clad policy for determining the size of a dog.

◆ Charge a flat fee. We prefer to pick one price point, in our case $9, and pack it with value. Additional dogs can be bathed at a reduced rate. We picked $5.

◆ Charge a flat fee with add-ons. You can use a standard base price and give the owner the option to upgrade the bath at your dog wash, maybe by using a premium shampoo or nail clippers or breath spray. With this method you can create a menu of washes for your customers.

HOW MUCH SHOULD I CHARGE?

Price is a function of your costs, the service you provide, your image and profit. With a dog wash you want to find a price that the market will bear - the highest price you can charge without driving customers away. This will largely be a guess on your part but you should err on the side of over charging. People make service choices on value, not price so make sure your service is perceived as valuable and you can justify your price.

Lower prices won't necessarily mean higher sales - they may be telling your customer that you don't believe your service is valuable. Low prices also mean you have to make more sales to reach revenue projections. And once you set a price, raising it is difficult.

Ultimately, your price will be based on feeling. People feel better if they sense that they are paying the right price for what they are getting. You will feel better if you know you are making a fair profit. Set your price so you do not regret it either way.

WHAT SHOULD I INCLUDE WITH THE WASH?

We include the choice of all 9 of our shampoos, combs, brushes, scrubbrushes, blowdryer, towels and a spritz of cologne and breath spray. In short, we include everything we have for one price. Some shops rent the facility and sell the shampoo. Some shops charge separately for the use of the bathing station and for the use of the grooming tools. By choosing a single price point with as much value as possible we believe we are not only pleasing the customer but mitigating against future competition. If we make certain the customer has a pleasant washing experience and they feel they are getting maximum value for their dollar, why would they go somewhere else?

HOW DO I CALCULATE THE MARK-UP ON MY RETAIL GOODS FOR SALE?

You must first decide how much mark-up, on the average, you will need from all your items to (1) cover the cost of your merchandise, (2) pay all your operating expenses, and (3) provide for a determined level of profit. The mark-up is the selling price less the cost of the goods.

The Grand Opening

WHAT SHOULD I DO FOR MY GRAND OPENING?

We do not recommend any grand opening celebrations. What if you spent $2000 to promote a grand opening celebration and 100 people show up with their dogs and you have room to wash only four at a time? We feel there are better ways to spend the scarce promotion dollar.

But you are proud of your new dog wash and you want to tell everybody about it and have a big grand opening party. If that is the case we suggest that you wait until you have been open for a month before the big blow-out to make sure all the kinks are out of your operation. Dream up special offers, have fresh-baked dog treats, games for the kids and dogs - if you do it, do it BIG, because you only have one chance for a grand opening.

You will want to make certain your inventories are full and all your signage is in place because these are your image. If you plan a media blitz, make sure you allow local editors as much lead time as possible.

But don't fixate on a "Grand Opening." Your entire promotional campaign (Section II) will be your Grand Opening over your first few months of operation.

WHAT IS A PROFESSIONAL OPEN HOUSE?

Once you have your operation running smoothly, you will want to plan an open house for veterinarians, trainers, pet sitters - any pet professionals you hope to establish relationships with. These relationships can take any form from casual mutual referrals to formal partnerships. Before a fellow pet professional will recommend your dog wash to one of his customers he will need to be suitably impressed with your operation.

Explaining The Business

WHAT IS THE "TOUR?"

The curiousity-seekers will start to come before you even open for business and they will keep coming even after you are an established operation. The people will want to know about your dog wash. You need to have a tour of your facilities prepared for when they knock on your door.

Be prepared to tailor your presentation to your prospect: Does she want to talk about her pet or is she in a hurry? Is he skeptical about your operation or think it is the best idea he's ever seen?

Conclude every tour by giving your visitor your business card and any take-away promotional material you have ready. You can also give a dog biscuit to take back home to the dog.

WHAT IS THE BEST WAY TO HANDLE PHONE REQUESTS FOR INFORMATION?

When people call your shop they will want to know:

- ◆ **Your Hours**
- ◆ **Your Prices**
- ◆ **Directions**
- ◆ **How It Works**

The two most important things to remember when answering the phone are:

1. Never give the price without telling the caller everything that it includes.

2. Have clear, easy-to-follow directions to your shop ready from every possible section of your trading area. You may want to type up these directions and have them by the phone. Get in your car and measure how far it is from all the important landmarks on the way to your shop. Your customers will appreciate it and remember your professionalism.

Everyday Operations

WHAT IS THE PROCEDURE WHEN A CUSTOMER BRINGS A DOG INTO THE SHOP?

If you do not recognize the owner or dog, ask if it is her first time to the shop. If so, show her to the bathing station and explain the procedure. Help with the pet step to get the dog into the tub. Let the customer know you are available to help and leave her on her own. If your shop is full when the customer arrives direct them to the waiting room and offer to bring out a brush for them to use while they are waiting.

After a few minutes, check back and make sure everything is going smoothly with the wash. We take photographs of every new dog being bathed and post the photos on the wall. People enjoy having pictures taken of their dogs and some will even stop by your shop to see the dog's picture before the next bath.

Record the demographic information of gender, age, dog size, and time of visit on the Demographic Matrix (see Section III). Also record the number of dogs and whether it is a repeat customer. This information will be crucial to knowing your business. If the customer has had a positive experience, casually point out your frequent bather's program (see Section II).

IS THERE ANYTHING I SHOULD KNOW ABOUT CLEANING UP?

You will want to develop a routine to clean up and prepare the bathing station as efficiently as possible, especially on busy days. Each tub should be wiped down and disinfected after each usage. Use a pail or plastic bag to collect hair from the tub and trap.

Cleaning will be the most important job you have to do in the shop. People will remember how clean your dog wash was long after they forget your friendliness and efficiency.

ARE THERE ANY ON-THE-JOB EMERGENCIES I CAN LOOK FORWARD TO?

The one emergency you can prepare for is a slow-draining tub. This will cause the water to back up and overflow the rack, forcing the dog to stand in water. An old-fashioned plunger will often free the drain enough to allow the water to escape. You can also have drain-clearing chemicals and other products on hand.

WHAT ABOUT A CUSTOMER WHO WANTS ME TO WASH HIS DOG?

The basic philosophy of a dog wash is that it is better for the dog to have its owner take command of the bathing chore. It defeats the purpose to do otherwise. Still, some owners will be physically unable to properly bathe their dog or unsure on how to do it. Others may just want someone else to do the wash. Unless you are a professional groomer or part of your business is full-time grooming, you will want to discourage this practice.

If you want to offer the service of washing dogs by yourself or staff, we suggest the following:

- Only offer the service on days when you will not be busy, for instance, weekday afternoons;
- Charge at least twice as much for this service - the purpose of a self-service dog wash is not to have the shop owner washing dogs, remember;
- Inform the owner that he will have to remain with the dog in the bathing station. You are certainly not going to be responsible for dogs left unattended in your shop;
- Have a waiver form available for the owner to agree to (Section III) in the event you will be doing the dog washing.

WHAT HAPPENS WHEN DOGS FIGHT?

You will find your customers to be responsible dog owners. They will have their dogs on short leashes, especially if they know their dog is not socialble. You may want to require all dogs to be on a leash but, as with a veterinarian's office, the dog is with the owner at all times in a dog wash.

SHOULD I REQUEST PAYMENT BEFORE OR AFTER THE DOG WASH?

It is to your advantage to have the customer pay for the dog wash after the bath as this increases the chance of having him buy some of your retail goods. Some customers will, however, want to pay ahead of time when their money is dry and so they can concentrate on washing the dog.

WHAT ABOUT TIPS?

Believe it or not, people will want to tip you. Although in most cases you have done little besides saying "hello" and good-bye," your customers will be so happy that your operation exists that they will want to tip you. In addition to thanking them for their generosity you might have a special treat for the dog handy when a tip comes your way.

If you go long enough without a bath,
even the fleas will leave you alone.
-James Thurber

Fleas

HOW DO I CONTROL FLEAS IN THE SHOP?

Fleas will not be a problem if you remain diligent. If a dog comes into your shop with a flea infestation be certain to vacuum and spray after his departure. Wear white socks or go in bare feet so you will know if any fleas are present immediately. Treat any potential flea areas immediately. Cleanliness is one of your biggest selling points and nothing will discourage a repeat visit faster than if a customer discovers fleas on his newly cleaned dog when he gets home.

SHOULD I OFFER FLEA DIPS?

During flea season, you will get many calls asking if you do flea dipping. If a shop has enough bathing stations, one can be set aside for chemical dips and medicated baths. But it is not a good idea to expose the general population of dogs to these tubs.

The fight is not always to the strongest
nor the race to the swiftest,
but that is the way to bet.
-Damon Runyan

Skunks

WHAT CAN I DO FOR CUSTOMERS WITH A "SKUNKED" DOG?

There are not many dogs who win a scrap with a skunk - and the biggest loser is usually the owner. Some dog wash owners who operate in rural areas and live close to the shop even offer a Skunk Hot Line for their customers so they can open the shop at any time of the day or night to treat a dog who has just met with a drenching of skunk spray.

Thsi is not a minor inconvenience that will go away on its own. The unlucky owner may be smelling that skunk every time her dog gets wet for up to two years!

When dealing with a skunked dog the owner must act immediately. Do not allow the skunk spray to dry. Wash the dog right away - any shampoo will do. Then you can attack with a de-skunking preparation. Mix a quart of 3 percent hydrogen peroxide with a 1/4 cup of baking soda. Add a teaspoon of plain shampoo and two tablespoons of Pet Odor Eliminator, if available. **Unfortunately, you can not prepare for disaster and pre-mix this solution for your customers as it builds up too much pressure in the container and will explode.**

And what about the old folk remedy of tomato juice? It may work or it may just stain the dog's coat red. Instead of a jar of V-8, stock a specially formulated deodorizing dog shampoo for the unfortunate victims.

Money will buy a pretty good dog,
but it won't buy the wag of his tail.
-Josh Billings

Petty Cash Management

WHY SHOULD I KEEP A PETTY CASH FUND?

Petty cash provides a systematic method for paying and recording out-of-pocket cash payments too small to be made by check. In addition to small amounts of postage and miscellaneous supplies, you will find a petty cash system handy in paying for film developing if you take pictures of all the dogs that come into your shop.

HOW DO I SET UP A PETTY CASH FUND?

Write a check payable to "Petty Cash" for $25. Cash the check and place the money in an accessible box. Keep a worksheet and pen in the box. Everytime you dip into the fund, record the date, payee and amount. You can also store receipts in the box. When the fund gets low, write another check and continue the procedure.

Use the petty cash as little as possible - only when there is no practical way to write a check. You should try and pay all your business bills by check so business expenses are easily recorded.

Maintain no more than $25 in the fund and discipline yourself not to use the petty cash for anything except necessary supplies. When you need to take money out of the business account for non-business use write a check for "cash" or payable to yourself and cash into a personal account. Never use the business account or petty cash fund for personal expenses because it becomes too confusing and doubles your bookkeeping.

SHOULD I ACCEPT CREDIT CARDS?

Credit cards are a convenience to your customers and an expense to you. Banks charge a fee depending on sales volume per month which can run as much as 5% per transaction. There is also a set-up fee and the rental of the imprinter.

Is it worth the expense? If you are just selling dog washes, probably not. Not many people are going to take their dog home if you won't take a credit card. But if you want to make $20 sales of merchandise or also have full-time grooming, it will begin to make sense to consider convenient charge cards.

Credit cards normally require between 30 and 60 days to establish. You can make arrangements through your own bank but shop around because transaction fees can vary from 1.5 to over 5 percent.

SHOULD I ACCEPT PERSONAL CHECKS?

This is a convenience you should afford your customers. What if a check bounces? In most cases, it is not intentional (we have had one bad check in 5 years). The reasons could be:

- **Insufficient Funds.** Contact the customer, indicating that you will redeposit the check. If it comes back a second time the bank will not accept a third try.
- **Account Closed.** The customer may have switched banks and made an honest mistake. Or it could be an intentional rubber check. To get payment you must contact the customer.
- **Stop Payment.** This is unlikely to happen as the cost of the stop payment is likely to exceed the value of the check, but if you encounter this situation you must also contact the customer to receive payment.

Maybe they call it take-home pay
because there is no other place you
can afford to go with it.
-Franklin P. Jones

Bookkeeping

SHOULD I KEEP MY OWN BOOKS?

Keeping your own books, even if only in a simplified manner, will provide the information that is essential to run your business. You must know how much it costs to open your door every day. Set aside a specific time each week to update your books, establish a system for saving receipts and recording expenses and this is not a dreary chore.

WHAT IS THE BEST METHOD TO USE?

For everyday use, a single entry system (see "Money In/Money Out" in Section III) is the simplest. For any transaction only one entry is made: either to income or as an expense. In this way you will be able to summarize and analyze all your financial activity - money coming in and money going out.

The single entry system will not provide a complete record of inventory on hand, outstanding debt and other integral parts of your business.

WHAT ABOUT PAYROLL?

There is no way aorund it - doing a payroll is a headache. Laws are always changing, reporting agencies seem to multiply by the month. If your business grows enough it will save you money to hire this unseemly chore out to a payroll service. Otherwise, check with your state agencies and they will gladly provide you with the armful of forms and applications that you will become well acquainted with as an employer.

Paperwork

WHAT DOCUMENTS SHOULD I HAVE ON HAND?

- **Articles, by-laws, partnership agreements.** Keep all documents which establish and define the business for as long as the business exists.

- **Names, addresses, social security numbers for all owners and stockholders.** Include date joined, date departed and level of participation. Keep as long as the business exists.

- **Record of owners' contributions and withdrawls.** Maintain a ledger of all financial contributions between the owners and the business. Keep as long as the business exists.

- **Minutes of board meetings.** Keep as long as the business exists.

- **Permits, licenses, insurance policies and leases.** Keep as long as these remain in force and an additional three years for the IRS.

- **Loan papers.** Keep as long as outstanding and another three years for the IRS.

- **Invoices, bills, sales receipts, cash receipts and credit memos.** Keep all day-to-day documents for three years for the IRS.

- **Complete data on all current and past employees.** This should include names, addresses, social security numbers, date hired, wage rates and dates of raises, payroll withholding, W-4 exemptions, injuries, workers' compensation claims, evaluations, date employment ended and why. These should be kept as long as the business exists.

- **Bank deposits, cancelled checks and bank statements.** Keep these for three years for the IRS.

- **Annual profit and loss and other financial statements.** Keep as long as the business exists. Although monthly statements are not required for the IRS, they should be kept to study your business roots.

- **Tax returns.** Keep a copy for each year the business exists.

- **Ledgers.** Keep as long as the business exists.

> *Dogs are better than human beings,*
> *because they know but do not tell.*
> *-Emily Dickinson*

Getting Customers To Come Back

HOW MUCH REPEAT BUSINESS CAN I EXPECT?

Repeat business and word of mouth advertising are the key to your business survival. You will hear it over and over again: "This is the easiest bath I have ever given my dog." If your price is fair and loaded with value, if your shop is clean, if you have provided friendly service - THERE IS NO REASON FOR THE OWNER NOT TO BRING THE DOG BACK.

You will find that 1/2 of your business is repeat business within six months. It is recommended that a healthy dog be bathed every six weeks or so; you will find many of your customers will develop a monthly schedule of visits.

How can you use these figures to establish sales goals? Say you want to average a very modest 3 new customers a day (about 20 a week). You will have a customer base of 1000 in a year. If you can make 650 of them repeat customers who have an average of five visits per year, you have over 4000 washes.

WHAT IS THE BEST WAY TO KEEP CUSTOMERS COMING BACK?

Your marketing and promotion (Section II) are your ongoing weapons in retaining customers. Everything you do should be done to minimize the opportunity for customer dissatisfaction.

Financial Documents

HOW MUCH WILL IT ALL COST?

That is up to you. You should be cutting costs by comparing vendors, looking for used equipment when possible and planning ahead. The theoretical documents on the following pages will help you plan your dog wash business according to your budget.

Capital Equipment List

MAJOR EQUIPMENT	MODEL	VENDOR	PRICE

Grooming Table
48"L x 24"W x 30"H

Shop Vacuum

Bathtubs
Dog Washing Tub (3)
Specialty Tub (1)

Spray Hose (4)

Hair Trap (4)

Tub Restraint (4)

Floor Decking

Lounge Furniture
Four chairs, table

Office Furniture
Desk, Files

Computer

Fax Machine/Telephone

Cash Register

Blowdryers (4)

Aprons (4)

Towels (72)

Washer/Dryer

Hot Water Heater

Bulletin Boards (2)

REPLACEABLE SUPPLIES	MODEL	VENDOR	PRICE

Brushes and Combs
Professional Mat Removing Rake
De-Matting Tool
Slicker Brush
Grooming Mitt
Bristle Brush
Pin Brush
Flea Comb
Curry Comb

Cologne (8 oz & refillable gallon)

Basic Shampoo (5 gal - 16:1)
Scented Shampoo (4 gal)
White Coat Shampoo (1 gal)
Black Coat Shampoo (1 gal)
Natural Shampoo (4 gal)
Oatmeal Shampo (4 gal)
Odor Neutralizer Shampoo (4 gal)
Creme Rinse (1 gal)
Flea & Tick Shampoo (5 gal)

Disinfectant (4 gal)

Treats Dog Biscuits - broken (20 lb)

Start-Up Expenses

Six Months Rent (+Security Deposit)	$7,000
Phone and Utility Deposits	$200
Office Equipment	$100
Signage	$700
Washing Stations	$3,000
Shop Supplies	$900
Inventory	$1,000
Promotional Push	$2,100
Licenses and Inspections	$400
Insurance	$300
Office Supplies	$100
Operating Expenses	$1,400
Total Start-Up Expenses	**$17,200**

Three-Year Income Projection

	Year One 75 Dogs/Week	Year Two 150 Dogs/Week	Year Three 200 Dogs/Week
Sales:			
Dog Washes	$39,000	$78,000	$104,000
Shop Sales	$5,400	$7,200	$9,000
Total Sales	**$44,400**	**$85,200**	**$113,000**
Cost of Materials	$585	$26,770	$1,560
Variable Labor	$15,600	$35,100	$52,000
Cost of Goods Sold	$3,000	$4,000	$5,000
Gross Margin	**$25,215**	**$43,430**	**$54,440**
Operating Expenses:			
Utilities	$1,800	$1,980	$2,400
Salaries	-----	$1,710	$3,420
Payroll Taxes/Benefits	-----	$154	$308
Advertising	$4,500	$9,000	$10,800
Office Supplies	$240	$400	$480
Insurance	$900	$900	$900
Maintenance	$300	$300	$300
Legal/Accounting	$650	$650	$650
Licenses	$375	$75	$75
Boxes/Paper	$120	$120	$240
Telephone	$360	$480	$600
Depreciation	$660	$660	$660
Miscellaneous	$300	$450	$600
Rent	$9,600	$9,600	$10,200
Total Expenses	**$19,805**	**$26,479**	**$31,633**
Net Profit (Loss) Pre-Tax	**$5,410**	**$16,951**	**$22,807**

Assumptions:
> **$10 per dog visit**
> **$.15 material per wash**

> **$4 Year One commission per dog; $4.50 Year Two; $5.00 Year Three**
> **Part-time Weekend Manager Hired Year Two and Three at $6/Hr for 19 weekends**
> **Addition of two washing stations and another blowdryer in Year Two**

First Year Income Projection

	Worst Case 50 Dogs/Week	Medium Case 75 Dogs/Week	Best Case 100 Dogs/Week
Sales:			
Dog Washes	$26,000	$39,000	$52,000
Shop Sales	$3,600	$5,400	$7,200
Total Sales	**$29,600**	**$44,400**	**$59,200**
Cost of Materials	$390	$585	$780
Variable Labor	$10,400	$15,600	$20,800
Cost of Goods Sold	$2,000	$3,000	$4,000
Gross Margin	**$16,810**	**$25,215**	**$33,620**
Operating Expenses:			
Utilities	$1,800	$1,800	$1,800
Salaries	-----	-----	-----
Payroll Taxes/Benefits	-----	-----	-----
Advertising	$3,600	$4,500	$5,400
Office Supplies	$240	$240	$240
Insurance	$900	$900	$900
Maintenance	$300	$300	$300
Legal/Accounting	$650	$650	$650
Licenses/Inspections	$375	$375	$375
Boxes/Paper	$120	$120	$120
Telephone	$360	$360	$360
Depreciation	$660	$660	$660
Miscellaneous	$300	$300	$300
Rent	$9600	$9600	$9600
Total Expenses	**$18,905**	**$19,805**	**$20,705**
Net Profit (Loss) Pre-Tax	**($2,095)**	**$5,410**	**$12,915**

Assumptions:
> **$10 per dog visit**   > **$4 commission per dog**
> **$.15 material per wash**

Starting and Running A Do-It-Yourself Dogwash

Section Two: Promoting Your Business

Starting And Running A Do-It-Yourself Dog Wash
Section Two: Promoting Your Business

Research

WHAT QUESTIONS SHOULD I ASK POTENTIAL CUSTOMERS WHO USE GROOMERS?

◆   How far do you drive to get to your groomer?

◆   Why did you choose this groomer?

◆   What do you have done?

◆   How often do you go?

◆   What are you willing to do yourself?

◆   How much does it cost?

◆   How long does it take?

◆   What do you like best about the groomer?

◆   What do you not like about the groomer?

◆   Does the dog enjoy the experience?

WHAT MATERIAL SHOULD I KEEP IN A COMPETITORS FILE?

Even before you open for business you will want to begin assembling a file of all the marketing activity by dog-related businesses in your trading area. Where are they advertising? How big are their ads? What events are they sponsoring? Collect all their flyers and other printed material. Make site visits and take notes. Keep this file current as you continue in business.

CENSUS TRACT DATA

Every ten years, by Constitutional decree, the United States does some of the most important market research a small business can get. The Census not only counts people, but records such useful tidbits as household income, type of housing, age and much more. All this information is available to the public and in selected libraries in every state, known as depositories.

The information is assembled by zip code and easily understood. Do you want to know what zip codes in your trading area contain the highest concentration of apartments (where it is difficult to wash dogs)? You can find such information in the Census Tracts. You can also get the data broken out in useful area maps.

The Census Tract data will help sharpen your knowledge of the trading area around your dog wash and direct your promotional efforts.

Some days you're the dog;
some days you're the hydrant.
-Unknown

Marketing Arsenal

The first thing people think when they think promotion is "advertising." We believe paid advertising is the *last* thing you should be considering when opening a dog wash. That is why you will find it dealt with last in this section of the manual.

Paid advertising is expensive and risky. Research has shown it requires as many as *twenty-seven* impressions before a prospect may be moved to respond to your message. You simply do not have that kind of money to spend to attract customers. The good news is that you do not have to rely on paid advertising to get business - it is simply a single marketing weapon you have at your disposal. As it is the most expensive weapon, we suggest you consider it last.

DOG WASH NAME

Ideally you want to choose a name that tells people what you do without explanation. We feel "**Dogomat**" is self-explanatory as a place to bring dogs to be cleaned and be cleaned by the owner. Maybe it works too well; people who have never heard of the self-service dog wash concept assume they are all called dogomats, like laundramats. In general, when birthing a name for your dog wash you should consider these factors:

◆ You want a name that is pleasant and easy to pronounce, not easily confused and memorable as yours alone.

◆ It should look and sound attractive: to people talking about your business, to customers you talk to on the phone, on your letterhead.

◆ Your name should accentuate the positive and avoid the negative.

- Your name should also not severely limit you as you grow and stand the passage of time. Also avoid tying your name to a fad or technology that may be extinct in a few years; Wells Fargo was able to ditch "Stagecoach Company" in its name, you may not be so lucky.
- It may be tempting with a dog wash to dream up a funny name. Avoid the temptation. What you think is funny and creative, your customers may not get.

Try your business name on people who you don't know well and don't know about your dog wash plans. Get their reaction in light of the above goals.

To register your name, go to the county office that handles fictitious names and ask to see an alphabetical listing of all names. If you find the name you want is already listed, check to see if it is current. If not, you can file an Abandonment of Fictitious Name Statement.

COLOR

Color is memorable. Think how many companies whose colors you can identify. Choosing colors for your business means not only interior and exterior paints but color schemes for your printed brochures and advertising. The following are examples of color shemes:

- **Monochrome.** This scheme relies on a single color. Two, three or more tints and shadings of this basic color are used.
- **Complementary Colors.** This plan combines any two colors that appear opposite one another on a "color wheel." Red/green, orange/blue, and violet/yellow are examples of complementary color schemes.
- **Triadic Colors.** This scheme uses three colors, all equidistant from one another on the color wheel: orange/green/violet or blue/yellow/red are examples.
- **Analogous Colors.** This approach focuses on a single color but uses some qualities from the colors immediately next to it on the color wheel. An example would be yellow-green/green/blue-green.

Dog Wash Business Names Across the County:

> U-Wash Doggie
> U-Wash Puppy
> Be the Groomer
> Bill's Doggie Bath 'O' Mat
> Wag & Wash
> Laund - UR - Mutt
> All Paws Pet Wash
> Bark-N-Splash Self-Serve Pet Wash
> Dippity Dog Self Serve Pet Wash
> Do-It-Yourself Pet Wash
> E Z Pet Wash
> Dingo & Sparkys Pet Wash
> My Dirty Paws Pet Wash
> Scrub A Dub Self Serve Pet Wash
> Poochies Self Service Pet Wash Espresso Bar
> Shampet Pet Wash
> U Do It Pet Wash Center
> U Suds Pet Wash
> You Dirty Dawg Pet Wash
> Dipsy Doodle Dog Wash
> Jean's Dog Wash
> Oggie Doggies Dog Wash
> Rub A Dub Dog Wash
> Smoochable Pooch You Wash Dog Wash
> U Bathe M Dog Wash
> Washadoggery Self Service Dog Wash
> Ye Old Dog Wash

Logo

You can spend thousands of dollars for a logo but not too many people are going to associate your graphic look with your business unless you can spend oodles of money to splash it everywhere. How many of the small businesses in your area have a logo? Probably not too many that you can remember. And how does it help their business?

If you have your mind set on a logo, you are best off looking for a generic symbol or, if possible, locate a student in a near-by art school to rustle up a design. Another inexpensive way to create a logo is to use distinctive typography for your dog wash name. Protect your logo by registering it with your state or with the United States Patent and Trademark Office.

Theme

Our theme is: **The Dogomat Equation: NO clean-up + No clogged drains + No sore backs = HAPPY owners + HEALTHY pets.** This not only describes our business philosophy but is the backbone of all our promotions. We use it in our print ads and radio commercials, it is on our main board in the shop and on our stationery and business cards. It is the hardest working promotional weapon we have.

Create a theme that summarizes the biggest benefits of your dog wash. Pick one you can use forever since the longer you use your theme the more your company image resonates with your customers.

Days & Hours of Operation

If you are open when your competition is not, you should gain extra business. In the beginning, you may want to let your customers choose your hours. By recording when people use your service over the first few months you will know the times when your shop is busiest. After analyzing this information, you may want to establish permanent hours.

PHONE DEMEANOR

Every time you answer the phone you are promoting your dog wash. You can win or lose people with the way you answer the phone. When someone asks for directions to your shop, have a precise and concise answer ready. You may even want to have written directions from different locations in your trading area posted by the phone. When someone asks for your prices don't just give a number - tell about everything that is included in that price.

TELEPHONE ANSWERING MACHINE

Keep your message short and informative. If you have the capacity, include testimonials. Remember that the customers you have are more important than the ones you may get so don't pick up the phone when dealing with a customer in the shop. Let the machine take it - and have your message state that, "if you call during our normal business hours and get this message, we are with a customer."

NEATNESS

You cannot keep your shop too clean. The cleanliness of your shop will be among your biggest selling points - and probably the first thing your customer comments on when talking up your shop.

WINDOW DISPLAYS

Do something to invite people inside. If you take photographs of the dogs being washed in your shop, make sure people can see all the dogs in the tubs through the window. Are you giving anything away? Or running a contest? Let the people on the street see it through your window.

SERVICE

Service is one of the primary reasons why a customer selects a particular business. Even though you are running a "self-service" operation there are countless ways for you to provide service to your customers. Help get the dog into the tub, provide extra towels, keep the shampoos filled. Nothing makes your business stand out like superior service.

FOLLOW-UP

In the early months of your business, send thank-you letters to each customer who visits your shop for the first time. In the letter is a self-addressed, stamped card asking for comments. Expect 25% to be returned - filled with invaluable testimonials and tips for running your business better. When you heed a suggestion and implement a change, let your tipster know about it. Nothing will cement a customer relationship faster than that level of involvement.

COMMUNITY INVOLVEMENT

Find out about the dog-related charity events in your area. Sponsor a local youth sports team. If you can't afford money for sponsorship, volunteer.

PERSONAL APPEARANCES

Volunteer to speak to schools and clubs about starting a business or working in the dog-business. If you are accomplished enough, try and teach a class at a local school in starting a business.

My dog is worried about the economy because Alpo is up to 99 cents a can. That's almost $7.00 in dog money.
-Joe Weinstein

Signs

INSIDE SIGNS

These do not need to be fancy printed messages but can be hand-written on chalkboards or dry erase boards which give a personal feel to your business. Signs can spur impulse purchasing, act as silent salespeople, inform and educate, and reinforce your company image.

You don't have that many retail items for sale; highlight as many as you can with their own promotional sign.

OUTSIDE SIGNS

These crucial promoters can be at your store or far away but they always must be directing people to your business. Before you decide on a size, get in your car and drive by your shop several times. Notice the first time on the street when your sign will actually be spotted by a passing motorist. What is competing with it? How big must it be to stand out? What else can you do to make it be seen?

With a dog wash, you must decide what is more important: your shop's name or the service, ie., a dog wash. We chose the latter. Being a new concept in our area, we felt it was more important that people knew *what* we did, not *who* we were. So we have three signs that indicate "dog wash" and only two with our "**Dogomat**" name.

Get your signs in play as early as possible. Hand paint an "Opening Soon" as soon as you take possession of your property and let it stand in until the big sign comes. And outside signs do not have to be confined to your building. How about a magnetic sign for your car?

Dogomat Promise

We clean and deodorize the bathing station after every wash.

Our disinfectant is effective against canine parvovirus, canine distemper, pseudorabies virus and Newcastle's virus.

Sample Inside Sign:

WOW!

Dogomat

Gift Certificates

Dog Wash
&
Gourmet Bag of Treats
Only

$10

Please Limit Your Blowdrying to 10 Minutes - Your Dog May Get Dehydrated!

BUSINESS CARDS

Make sure there is more than a name, address, telephone number on your card. Print your theme, hours, benefits, a map - anything you can think of to turn your business card into a mini-brochure. Use both sides of the card. Do things to make people want to keep your card: include an inspirational quote or a good joke or brain-teaser. How about a useful dog tip such as how to remove paint from a dog? Or a place to write emergency dog-related numbers. Or steps to administer first aid to dogs? The possibilities are endless.

Place stacks of your business cards on display in your shop for customers to take home and pass along. You can hand them out to anyone you meet. Leave them on the table at the restaurant with the tip. Leave them in library books. Drop them in outgoing mail such as local bills. Leave them everywhere your prospects may see them.

When designing your cards you want to achieve instant readability. Keep your design free of clutter and breathing with plenty of "white space." Make your business cards consistent with all your other printed material.

If your budget allows, consider some of the innovative ways people are now using business cards. Some of these include the double-size card which can fold over, the photograph card and the printed Rolodex card.

When ordering, obtain quotes from several printers as business card prices are extremely variable from shop to shop. Order cards in quantities of 1000 or more to keep your costs as low as possible.

BROCHURES

The brochure you will create is an informational brochure: something to mail when information is requested and for prospective customers to take away when they have stopped in your shop for a tour. You won't be able to afford fancy four-color brochures on slick paper but you can still create a professional promotional piece that will represent your shop well in your trading area.

If you have access to a computer and printer, you can take advantage of specially designed colored brochure papers. These papers cost less than $10 for 100 sheets making the cost of your brochures less than a dime each. You will only need a few hundred of these brochures as distribution will be limited to visitors to the shop, callers requesting information you can't answer over the phone and in press kits.

If you are not confident in your design abilities, use one of the many computer programs available to provide a template for your brochure. Or hire a designer. *Your brochure must look professionally designed.* Include visuals when possible. Brochures that are well-written and well-designed create an aura of credibility about your shop. Remember, your brochure is selling your shop when you are not around.

When writing copy for your brochure, concentrate on the **benefits** of the dog wash as covered in Section I: no clean-up, ease of bathing, affordability, etc. Tell people how your shop will solve their dog-washing problems. Endorsements and testimonials will be your strongest copy points so obtain them as soon as possible. Ask a satisfied customer for an endorsement to use in your promotion. They'll be glad to give it and you'll be happier to use it.

Include all the important information to enable customers to reach you: telephone numbers, e-mail address, street address. Absolutely include a map with your shop location starred. You may also want to include written directions. Also do not forget your hours of operation.

Anticipate all the questions anyone might have about your dogwash. Then answer them in your brochure.

STATIONERY

Very often, the look and feel of your stationery is the first impression made by your shop. People will see your envelope first, then your letterhead. Use the most expensive paper you can afford; a 100-percent cotton stock costs about a penny a sheet more than a standard bond. Colored inks and colored papers; a burgundy on ivory; for instance, can give your shop an upscale look for very little extra money.

As with business cards, get your stationery working for you with more than name-address-phone. Include your theme or top selling points on your letterhead.

ORDER FORM/INVOICE

People expect to see a standard invoice if they order something from you. Don't be standard. Like all your business forms, this is an opportunity to gain more business. Use your invoice to promote your service and highlight special products.

Make your forms as simple to understand as possible. If it is an order form, fill it out yourself to make sure there are no snags for a potnetial customer. Make it easy to do business with you.

Man is a dog's idea of
what God should be.
-Holbrook Jackson

Publicity

Getting publicity for your new dog wash will be about the easiest public relations job you will ever have. The press needs stories and yours has just about everything they love in a story: "quirky" new business, dogs, photo opportunities. Within a week of sending out our initial press release we were on our way to five newspaper articles, two television stories, radio coverage and one magazine piece - without a single follow-up call. Every media outlet in our market covered the opening of our dog wash.

Publicity is far more valuable to your dog wash than any paid advertising. Editorial coverage is more credible than advertising and people will remember "that article in the paper" months later. Chances are, if they don't call or visit immediately, they may rip out the story and file it for the future.

You will be making that story last forever as well. Cut out the news stories on your dogwash and post them on your bulletin board for customers to see. Reprint the stories and use them in all your future promotional mailings.

Your publicity efforts won't end with your Grand Opening Announcement. Many times your local paper will be interested in a follow-up story six months down the road on how that "new dog wash is doing." Announce anything of importance in your dog wash in the media.

It will never be as easy to get coverage again as it will be with your Grand Opening so be prepared to make follow-up calls. It may become frustrating since the trade-off for this "free advertising" is a lack of control, but your efforts will be rewarded many times over.

THE PRESS KIT

You do not have to be a public relations pro to get your shop publicity - your new dog wash is more important than how you present it. The following items will make up your Press Kit:

♦ **Press Release.** This is the heart of your publicity offering. It should be a maximum of two pages and should contain at least one quote from you, the founder of the dog wash, and one from a customer (even if it is your neighbor when you don't have any testimonials yet). Write in short, descriptive sentences but don't panic if you are not a writer - the reporters will write their own stories. Just describe your business in as clear a manner as possible.

Double-space your press release and give it a date. Write "For Immediate Release" on the top. List a contact person (yourself) with a phone number and address it to a specific editor or producer - phone the target newspaper or television station and ask for the appropriate person's name. Give your press release a headline, big and centered, and if you want to speak the journalist's language, end your press release with a "30" or "###," which is how they end articles. See the sample on pages 23.

♦ **Your Biographical Profile.** On your letterhead, print up a brief profile of your accomplishments and background. Keep it to one page.

♦ **Black and White Glossy Photographs.** If you have them, include a photograph of a happy customer washing a dog and, if you desire, one of yourself. The media will send their own photographers to your shop but yours may be used as well.

♦ **Testimonial Sheet.** When you collect written testimonials from customers, you will also get their permission to release their comments to the press. When you have them, send them in your kit.

♦ **Copies of Other Articles About Your Shop.** If you have any previous articles, include them in your kit.

Assemble everything in a logical order with the press release on top. Do not worry about fancy presentation folders - you can't afford them and you won't need them. Don't just send your kit to the biggest newspaper and television station in your region. Make it your business to know all the media in your trading area: local cable television programs, community newspapers, college newspapers. Follow-up in a week with a casual call to ask if your materials were received. But don't be surprised if you are already being interviewed by then.

BEING INTERVIEWED

Be prepared. Before reporters come to your shop, write out the key points you want to convey about your new dog wash. Take control of the interview so that no matter what the reporter asks, you can weave your key points into the answers.

As you prepare for your interview, keep your customers in mind. What do you want people to know about your business? When the questions come, focus on one or two points. Keep your answers brief and informative.

In your preparation for the interview, make the reporter's job easy by having entertaining anecdotes ready. If you have an informative quote, don't be afraid to use it with every interview.

Be positive and enthusiastic about your new venture; don't try to sell your business, the dog wash will sell itself.

Before the reporter leaves, make sure you have provided all the printed material you have available. If your shop has a tricky name, make sure the reporter has the correct spelling.

After the article appears or the television piece runs, make sure to send a complimentary thank-you to the reporter. It won't be every day she receives one of those.

SAMPLE PRESS RELEASE:

It is hard to tell who's happier with the opening of the **Dogomat** Do It Yourself Dogwash on Route 1 - New Castle County pets or their owners.

"I come in here and wash Max without getting myself all dirty and wet," laughs Billy Blue, as he blow-dried his high-spirited Gordon Setter. "This place is great. Max loves it and I can do it in a hurry."

Self-service pet washes have been popular on the West coast and in the midwest for more than a decade as dog owners seek an escape from clogged drains, wrenched backs and messy clean-up on Fido's bath day. Now Delaware dog owners have the same opportunity.

Bathing, especially for older and infirm dogs, can be extremely stressful on pets. At a self-service pet wash the only hands a dog feels are its owners.

The **Dogomat** is equipped with tubs elevated to waist level; an easy-to-use ladder allows the dogs to walk directly into the tub. Once inside the animal stands on a rack so its feet do not rest in chilly, dirty water. A chain secures the pet to the tub and long hoses reach all areas of the dog. Soothing warm water is delivered through one of five settings on a spray nozzle.

The cost for a basic wash at the **Dogomat** is $9, which includes a choice of 8 shampoos, including flea and tick products, towels, a professional pet dryer, brushes, combs, an apron and a spritz of after-bath cologne. Pet owners can also use the grooming table and clip unruly toenails. Following each bath the **Dogomat** cleans and disinfects the washing station. Additional dogs can be washed for $5.

The **Dogomat** is not just for dogs. The facilities can accomodate all sorts of critters: cats, monkies, pot-bellied pigs, parrots, iguanas, ferrets and rabbits.

The Canine Cafe at the **Dogomat** offers the widest selection of gourmet dog treats in the area. The tail-wagging menu of all-natural dog treats includes bagels, cookies, pizza, biscuit mixes, truffles and the one-of-a-kind Doggie Salad Bar. Eat in or carry out.

The **Dogomat** is located on Route 1 and is open Monday-Wednesday 11-8 and Friday-Sunday 9-6. For more information contact the **Dogomat** at 302-555-5555.

#

Did you ever walk into a room and
forget why you walked in?
I think that is how dogs
spend their lives.
-Sue Murphy

Low Cost Promotions

CIRCULARS

DESCRIPTION:

The use of circulars to advertise goes back to painting on cave walls. In American Colonial days posters were known as broadsides. Circulars can be distributed anywhere you think your customers may be: handed out to people at dog-related events, placed on car windshields, dropped into your mailings.

You will want to plan a "thumb-tack attack" by scouting out possible bulletin boards in your trading area on which you will want to keep your circulars posted. Possible locations include shopping centers, grocery stores, libraries, college campuses, and pedestrian malls.

When writing your copy for a posted circular keep your copy brief and develop as strong a headline as possible. Use color to enable your cicular to "pop" from a crowded bulletin board.

MEDIA:

◆ bulletin boards

COST:

◆ printing circulars

SAMPLE CIRCULAR:

DOGWASH OPENS!!!

DELAWARE'S FIRST!

DO IT YOURSELF AT

The Dogomat

THE DOGOMAT EQUATION:

NO clean-up + *NO* clogged drains + *NO* sore backs =
Happy Owners + Healthy Pets

GIVE YOUR DOG A STRESS-FREE BATH FOR JUST $9

You get your choice of 9 shampoos and finish with a free spritz of cologne.
You get full use of brushes, combs, blowdryers and towels. Strap on a rubber apron and give it a try!
AFTERWARDS YOU CAN REWARD YOUR PET WITH A TREAT FROM THE LARGEST SELECTION OF GOURMET DOG TREATS IN THE AREA!
One-of-a-kind **DOGGIE SALAD BAR** - eat in or carry out!
CATS, FERRETS, RABBITS, MONKEYS, POT-BELLY PIGS, PARROTS AND OTHER PETS ALL WELCOME!
Additional pets can be bathed for only $5.

INTERESTED PARTIES ARE INVITED TO INQUIRE AT THE OFFICES OF

Corporate Memberships

DESCRIPTION:

Large employers in your trading area like to offer small perks for their workers - especially if they don't cost anything. Contact the Benefits Manager from these companies and offer a discount, between 5 and 20%, for their employees. You will join their roster of local merchants and they will advertise your dog wash in employee newsletters and elsewhere. The existence of your dog wash shop will be made known to hundreds and even thousands of people. The cost of this valuable advertising is a dollar or two off your dog wash price.

If you really want to get ambitious with this promotion, you can charge a fee for a corporate membership and offer a steeper discount.

MEDIA:

   ◆   personal letters to Employee Benefits Managers

COST:

   ◆   postage
   ◆   stationery and envelopes, brochures

CORPORATE MEMBERSHIP OFFER LETTER:

In today's scramble for talented workers it seems companies are getting more and more creative when designing employee benefit plans.

I've noticed one strategy being used to appeal to employees is "dog friendly." Dogs are even showing up in offices and cubicles at some businesses. We have a way for you to be "dog friendly" without the mess.

It's the **Dogomat** Corporate Membership. Before I go any further, perhaps you haven't heard of the **Dogomat**. We are a new Do-It-Yourself Dog Wash in the area; the enclosed brochure and newspaper articles will tell you more about us.

With the Corporate Membership, we will give your employees the opportunity to wash their dogs for only $7.50 - almost 20% off the regular price of $9. All they need to do is show their employee identification card. We do not offer discounted rates and this Corporate Membership will be the only way to get a dog wash for $7.50.

No more chasing the dog around the backyard with a hose...
No more washing the dog in the same tub as the kids...
No more cleaning up a blizzard of hair in the bathroom...
No more frantic calls to the plumber to unclog drains...
No more calling in sick because of a sore back...
No more smelly dogs...

Well, you get the idea. The introductory Corporate Membership is good for six months. If you are interested, please call me at 555-5555.

DISCOUNT DAYS

DESCRIPTION:

You see gas stations offering cents-off days on certain weekdays; golf courses charge more to play on weekends than weekdays. You may want to run this type of promotion as well.

You will be busier on weekends than weekdays and to smooth out traffic flow in your shop you can offer a reduced rate on certain weekdays. This will encourage those owners who can use your shop on Tuesday afternoon to come during a slow time.

Do not be quick to use this promotion unless you are being overwhelmed at certain times - if you have packed your price with value your customers will feel they are getting a bargain any time they visit your shop.

MEDIA:

◆   in-store signage

COST:

◆   none

THE FAX MACHINE

DESCRIPTION:

Using the fax machine as an advertising medium is controversial and even illegal in some conditions. But when it is used locally it costs you nothing to send so you may want to consider it. When you open for business, simply fax a Grand Opening flyer or newsletter into your trading area. Fax numbers can be obtained in local business directories. Include a special offer for those bringing the fax into your shop so you can track results.

If you decide to use the fax machine we suggest the following:

◆ Transmit your fax on weekends and after business hours so you do not tie up another businesses' fax machine.

◆ Only fax your advertisement once.

◆ Include a disclaimer such as "if no one in your office owns a dog, we apologize for this inconvenience." Some people may be angry that you have "wasted their paper" with your fax but you'll get ten customers happy to learn about your service for every negative response. You will also find your fax has been copied and passed around some offices.

MEDIA:

◆ fax machine

COST:

◆ none

FREE WASHES FOR SHELTERS

DESCRIPTION:

Contact the local animal shelters in your area and offer a free dog wash as a reward for every new adoption. This will not only enhance their adoption package but it gives new dog owners an opportunity to sample your service. An average-sized shelter can have 2,000 adoptions a year which gives you an excellent way to expand your customer base. Of course, you will want to capture the names and addresses of these "freebies" to add to your mailing list and give you every opportunity to turn them into regular customers.

MEDIA:

- ◆ personal letters to shelter managers
- ◆ personal visits to shelters

COST:

- ◆ the overhead expense incurred in a single wash

SAMPLE PROPOSAL LETTER TO SHELTERS OFFERING FREE DOG WASHES:

We are a new Do-It-Yourself Dogwash which has recently opened on Route 1. The attached material will tell a little about our service.

We would like to offer a free dog wash as a "reward" to people adopting a new dog. We could just have people show the adoption papers or if you wanted to collect a small donation for the service we will provide FREE dog wash cards similar to the one attached. The value of the dog wash is $9 and the Delaware SPCA could sell them for a dollar or two to raise funds. To be redeemed the card need simply be filled out and initialed by a Delaware SPCA official.

If you have any interest in setting up a program of this type, please contact me at 555-5555.

Thank you for your time and consideration afforded this proposal.

FREQUENT BATHER'S CLUB

DESCRIPTION:

This is a common promotion whereby the regular customer is rewarded with a free dog wash after a certain number of visits. We call our club the Tailwaggers Club and give the free wash after five visits. Rather than use punch cards we keep track of the customer's visits. This way they do not have to worry about the hassle of keeping track of the little card or having it with them when they come to the dog wash. You will also capture their name on the application for your house mailing list (see Section III).

In addition to the free dog wash we offer Tailwaggers Club members 10% off all dog treats and supplies and a free subscription to our newsletter, the *Wash and Wag Rag*. We ask for the dog's birthday on the application and send out annual birthday cards.

MEDIA:

◆   in store signs

COST:

◆   none

FUNDRAISERS

DESCRIPTION:

During times when your shop is not open for business, make it available for community fundraisers. The organization running the fundraiser would be responsible for providing the dog washers, advertising the event and handling the money. Take a nominal amount for each dog washed to cover expenses (we take $4) and the organization, which can charge $15 or $20 or more for the service, keeps the remainder. Church groups, schools, youth organizations and others can raise several hundred dollars - and have fun - with this unique fundraising event. In addition to participating in your community, opening your shop to fundraisers is a good way to spread your name across town.

MEDIA:

- personal letters to group leaders
- press releases

COST:

- postage
- stationery and envelopes, brochures

LETTER TO SOLICIT FUNDRAISERS:

Raise money by washing dogs! At the **Dogomat**.

The **Dogomat** is a new self-service dogwash int he area; the enclosed brochure and newspaper articles will tell you about us.

The shop is closed on Thursday but I will be making the facilities available after 4:00 p.m. to student and youth groups to wash dogs as a fundraiser. We will supply all the shampoo, scrub brushes and towels and will also give your student dog washers a quick course on executing the ideal dog bath.

At the **Dogomat** we charge $19 to wash a dog regardless of size; your students can charge at least that much, if not more since it will be going to a good cause. All we ask is $4 per dog to cover expenses. With three bathing stations the students could wash as many as 8-10 dogs per hour, depending on how well they promote their event. So the potential is there to make several hundred dollars - not a tremendous amount but it has to be more fun than washing cars.

If you are interested in reserving a future Thursday to use the **Dogomat** as a fundraiser - or would like further information - please contact me at 555-5555.

PRESS RELEASE TO ANNOUNCE FUNDRAISERS:

The **Dogomat** self-service dogwash, makes its facilities available to schools, youth groups and community organizations every Thursday to use as a fundraiser. The **Dogomat** features waist-high, stainless steel bathing stations equipped with 6-foot hoses for efficient, stress-free bathing. The **Dogomat** provides aprons, shampoos, scrub brushes, blowdryers, towels and will also instruct your volunteer dog washers how to execute the "perfect" dog bath. For more information on how your organization can raise money with a dog wash at the **Dogomat** call 555-5555.

GIFT CERTIFICATES

DESCRIPTION:

Your customers will welcome the chance to give gift certificates to your dog wash. It is a unique - and practical - gift for a holiday, birthday or to welcome a friend's new dog to the home. Gift certificates help you by spreading the word about your service and propping up your cash flow, since the dog wash is paid for ahead of time.

Preparing personalized gift certificates if you have a computer is a snap. Design a template and whenever a gift certificate is purchased you simply type in the recipient dog's name and print. You can also purchase pre-printed gift certificates from stationery stores and fill in the blanks.

We include a small bag of treats to enhance the value of the gift certificate. Also provide your brochure and any other printed material so the recipient can find your shop.

MEDIA:

- in store signs
- newsletter

COST:

- none

HOUSE MAILING LIST

DESCRIPTION:

Keeping an existing customer and increasing your business with him is far, far easier than finding a new customer. Your house list will be your own personal gold mine. Start your customer mailing list on the day you open and never stop collecting names.

You can build your house list these ways:

◆   Run a contest. Name a mascot, or just have a monthly drawing for a free wash.
◆   Copy the address from anyone who pays by check.
◆   Install a SUGGESTIONS box.
◆   Place a Guest Book on your counter and invite visitors to sign in.
◆   Create a new customer starter's kit that may contain coupons, tip sheets on bathing and grooming, etc.

MEDIA:

◆   in store signs

COST:

◆   none

Newsletter

DESCRIPTION:

An informative single-page newsletter will be one of your most versatile promotional tools. Use it to sell your dog wash service, educate prospects about the concept and inform customers about important happenings in your business. Pack your newsletter with short, interesting copy that people will find useful - don't just pitch your dog wash to the exclusion of all else.

Your newsletter does not need to be slick to be effective. Keep these tips in mind:

- Produce a new newsletter regularly, once a quarter is plenty.
- Include your phone number and hours with every issue.
- Make an offer that will save readers money.
- Spend time to proofread your newsletter; like all your printed material it will be a reflection on your dog wash.
- You can save money by establishing a template design for your newsletter and pre-printing the standard elements in color. Add your black-and-white copy when you print the newsletter and you will have the impact of a two-color publication without the cost.
- Make your customers an important topic. Have any of your regular dogs just had puppies? Won any show awards? People love to see their names - and their dog's name - in print.

MEDIA:

- in store distribution
- mailed to house list

COST:

- printing
- postage

SAMPLE NEWSLETTER:

Wash and Wag Rag

Monday-Wednesday 11-8
Friday-Sunday 9-6

Summer 1998

Do-It-Yourself DogWash Opens In Delaware

Another Bath Day For The Dog At Your House?

Dogomat is Home of the Original Doggie Salad Bar

The tail-wagging menu of all-natural dog treats at The Dogomat includes cakes, cookies, pizzas and donuts - all woofingly endorsed by our official taster, Rockford - is the largest in the Tri-state area. Carry out or eat in at our one-of-a-kind Original Doggie Salad Bar.

Dogomat on Route 4 NOW OPEN

It's hard to tell who's happier about the opening of **The Dogomat** -The Do-It-Yourself Dogwash - New Castle County pets or their owners.

"I come in here and wash Max without getting myself all dirty and wet," laughs Tom Madden as he vacuums his high-spirited Gordon Setter dry. "This place is just great. Max loves it and I can do it in a hurry."

At the Dogomat, owners can escape the mess of bathing a dog in the house - quickly and economically. Waist-high washing stations get the job done without back strain.

For dogs (cats and other pets are welcome as well), a trip to The Dogomat is a stress-free adventure as they are tended to by the familiar hands of their owners.

The Dogomat - What's It All About

The cost for a basic wash at **The Dogomat** is $9 which includes:

- *unlimited time* in the bathing station
- brushes and combs
- choice of 8 shampoos
- blowdryer and towels
- rubber apron
- a spritz of cologne

Additional pets can be bathed for $5. If you want us to do it, we'll wash your dog for an additional $5. And, as always, the smiles are FREE!

A Healthy Dog Should Be Bathed Every 6 Weeks

The Dogomat
109 Main Street (Route 4)
Stanton
(next to the Dairy Queen)

Route 141 · Kirkwood Highway · Route 7 · Route 4 · I-95

The Dogomat Equation: NO clean-up + NO clogged drains + NO sore backs = Happy Owners + Healthy Pets

SPECIAL EVENTS

DESCRIPTION:

Staging a unique event will draw attention to your operation. When you plan a special event it gives you an opportunity to issue a press release. Often a special event will be the keystone of a coordinated effort of many of the promotional weapons at your disposal.

What are some of the special events you can plan? You are only limited by your imagination. Here are some:

- Celebrity Dog Wash
- Singles Night
- Photo Day
- Dog Portraits
- Dirtiest Dog Contest

MEDIA:

- in store signs
- press releases
- circulars
- newspapers
- newsletter
- radio

COST:

- advertising
- event preparation

TEAM BUILDING

DESCRIPTION:

You can multiply your promotional power byindentifying non-competing dog-related busi-nesses in your trading area and banding together. These can be kennel operators, pet sitters, dog trainers, veterinarians, small pet stores or doggie day care centers. Suddenly, advertising that was beyond your reach financially becomes affordable when split four or five ways.

There are many opportunities for joint promotions:

- co-sponsor a dog-related event
- produce a direct mail package with a flyer from each of the businesses
- mutual customer referrals
- pooling mail lists
- taking out a booth at local trade shows, business fairs and the like

Bring team members on one by one, seeking individuals whose goals and business beliefs are compatible with yours. Decide on an equitable divison of responsibilites because nothing will sour a business network faster than one member who feels as if she is not benefitting equally. Go slowly and build your team wisely; do more than is expected of you; follow up on referrals and you will be on your way to a successful team relationship.

MEDIA:

- personal contacts

COST:

- none

TESTIMONIAL BOOK

DESCRIPTION:

Create a booklet of your best testimonials. Ask for testimonials directly and tell customers you are compiling a testimonial book. More than likely they will be pleased and flattered to contribute.

Assemble a first-class booklet and send them to customers, prospects and the media. Use the testimonials in your print ads and brochure. Put the testimonials on your shop walls for your customers to see.

These testimonials will power your advertising copy. Your testimonials will go a long way in convincing skeptical prospects to try your dog wash, which will probably be a new concept in your community.

MEDIA:

- all printed material
- radio commercials
- answering machine

COST:

- none

EXAMPLES OF TESTIMONIALS:

"Great! What a unique, long over-due idea! A must for dog-owners -especially for those big, long-haired canines! Our first visit - a real plus - hope it continues!"
    - Brad & Diane & Lexus

"Great! I've told several people about the wonderful experience we had at the Dogomat. What a great idea! We hope you are there for along time. We will be back soon! Thank you!"
    - The Youngs & Carli

"Greatest idea since sliced bread. Dog feels more comfortable being bathed than having a groomer do it! Will probably use this service once a month because of its affordability."
    - Lucas & Winston

"I think your place is great! Having 4 dogs, bath time became a very frustrating and wet task! Your place made it much more enjoyable - for me and the dogs. If you ever need help, give me a call."
    - Gayle & Chip & Storm & Salena & Chesa

"A great set-up!"
    - Robert & Beach Boy & Sunny

"Having been a recent heart transplant patient your Dogomat allowed me to pamper my dog Simba with an easyness I need to have at this time. I will be back again and will refer my friends! We wish you all the best with this long overdue type of business. P.S. - Simba loved "the cats" at the 'Doggie Salad Bar!'"
    - Mark & Simba

"Sassy and I enjoyed her visit to the Dogomat and I enjoy the way she still smells."
    - Sara & Sassy

"Long needed service. My dog enjoyed his bath. See you soon."
    - Ed & Chauncy

"This business is a great idea. I used to spend $40 to bathe my dog (a Samoyed). Now I can go here and have four baths for the price of 1. Great idea. I was very impressed at how clean things are. We will absolutley be back!"
    - Heather & Yuri

"We love it. It keeps our bathroom clean."
    - Mel & Adam & Blizzard

"I will return again and again. Very clean!"
    - Lorie & Samie & Bea

"We thought it was great! Our Weimaraner, Luke, is usually a monster at bath time - but he was really good! We wer very impressed and will definitely be back! Thanks!"
    - Chris & Valerie & Luke

"We think your concept is great - Max will have no more baths at home or expensive trips to the groomer. We have told many people how wonderful your place is - we'll definitely be back!"
    - Tony & Max

"We really liked the deodorizing shampoo and hair dryers that didn't get really hot. Even though we named our dog Sneakers we don't want him to smell like one! We had a fun time."
    - Christine & Sneakers

"This is a great service and a real creative idea. I've told everyone I know about it. It makes a difficult job giving my 60-pound dog a bath more loving and pleasant."
    - Joann & Jasmine

"Kyla enjoyed her bath and goodies. We found the Dogomat to be very clean and a convenient way to keep her smelling and looking good. What a friendly place and helpful. We WILL be back."
    - Francine & Kyla

WORD OF MOUTH

DESCRIPTION:

Your customers will be your best salespeople. It is possible to build a business completely on the referrals of satisfied customers. How do you get it?

- ◆ **Do an extraordinary job.** People love to be the first to discover "the next hot product" or "the great new service." Be that "great service" and your customers will hardly be able to wait to get home and tell their dog-owning neighbor. We have had people call friends on their cell phones *while they were washing their dog* to tell about the great new place they have found.

- ◆ **Ask for it.** When a customer tells you how much he enjoyed washing his dog in your shop, don't be afraid to ask him to tell his friends.

- ◆ **Give your marketing material to your new customers as they leave.** This will not only reinforce their wise decision to come to your dog wash in the first place but they will likely pass the information along.

MEDIA:

- ◆ none

COST:

- ◆ none

Advertising

Newspapers

Collect as much information as you can on all the newspapers in your trading area: the daily newspaper; the local college newspapers; the free presses; the shopper's guides - whatever you have. Call and ask for a media kit.

Determine the circulation of the paper and the rates for advertising on different sized ads. Divide the total cost of the ad by the circulation and you will get the Cost Per Thousand, or CPM. This is your base measurement for how much it costs to reach 1000 readers.

When negotiating for space, insist on getting your ad placed on a right-hand page, above the fold. Research shows it will be more likely to be seen here.

When you decide which of your local papers is your best buy, buy as big an ad as you can afford. Generally, a half-page ad draws about 67% of the readership of a full-page ad. Most of your ads will certainly be smaller than 1/4 page. Here are some tips for ads less than 1/4 page:

- ◆ Make certain you have the right publication; look for ads like yours.
- ◆ Make sure your ad makes your shop obvious. Use a graphic or powerful headline to capture attention quickly.
- ◆ Use a border, your ad will seem much bigger.
- ◆ Make it easy for the reader to take advantage of your offer.
- ◆ Run the ad for as long a time as you can afford; it may take a reader six or more times seeing your ad to be comfortable enough to respond to it.

Make sure your ad has a strong headline; if the reader doesn't stop for your headline the meat of your pitch will surely never be read. Show a picture if possible. Include testimonials and emphasize the word FREE if you can. Make an offer and make it timely - get the reader to want to come to your shop.

If you do not want to design your own ad, the paper will do it for you. However your ad gets created, observe these rules:

- Use upper- and lower-case letters since ALL CAPS ARE HARD TO READ.
- Avoid using reverse type (white on black) anywhere in your ad.
- Sans serif type (without little feet) should be used only in headlines.
- Stay with one typeface for headlines and one for body copy.
- If you use a coupon, do it with dashes rather than dots.

CLASSIFIED ADS

Again, we suggest using costly newspaper advertising sparingly. You will get more bang for your buck if you schedule newspaper advertising to coincide with other promotions or if you know you will be getting publicity articles. The cumulative impact is far greater than a newspaper ad run in a promotional vacuum.

A cheaper way to do this "awareness advertising" is with classified ads. They will enable you to maintain a presence in your local paper inexpensively. These are considerations for classified ads:

- Use a headline, print it in capital letters and keep it short.
- Don't use abbreviations unless you know everyone will understand you.
- Include a way to contact the shop.
- Test different categories (Notices, Pets, etc.) to find the best one.
- Test different days of the week, some days are far more effective than others.
- Test long ads and short ads; short ads are not necessarily worth the savings.

Radio

Radio is best used when you have a special event to promote; the station may even be involved as a sponsor of your event. Like newspapers, its impact will increase if you run radio spots in tandem with other promotions.

Radio is the most targetted of all media. Each station is programmed to appeal to a specific demographic. The station representatives will tell you who they reach. Although radio spots are relatively inexpensive you will need to buy an extensive "flight" of commercials before you will make an impact on your intended customers.

Do not try to do too much when creating your radio commercial, which the station will write and produce for you if desired. Have one goal in mind. Repetition is the key.

Another way to use radio - or local cable television - is to start your own program. You buy the time and can fill it with your own programming. You can even sell advertising to make a profit on the program. This is most effective if you have teamed up with other dog businesses. There is no reason you can't have your own local "Doggie Hour."

SAMPLE RADIO SPOT:

60 Second Dogomat Radio Spot

HEADLINE (Ominous voice with reverb):

       New businesses to watch.

VOICE 1:   The Dogomat Do-It-Yourself Dogwash and Canine Cafe. Call 555-7721...

VOICE 2:   Or as the Brits say, triple-five, double-seven, two-one.

VOICE 1:   ...conveniently located on Route 1 where you get The Dogomat Equation - NO clean-up + NO clogged drains + NO sore backs = HAPPY owners + HEALTHY pets.

VOICE 2 (insistent):   Triple-five, double-seven, two-one.

VOICE 1 (world-weary voice, sardonically dripping with condescencion from every syllable):
       Yes, I heard you the first time. Very clever. (slips back to informative voice) For $9 you wash your dog with a choice of 8 shampoos, use of brushes and combs, a blowdryer and towels and a free spritz of cologne.

VOICE 2:   Just $9.

VOICE 1:   The Dogomat, home of the Original Doggie Salad Bar.

VOICE 2:   18 all natural gourmet dog treats.

VOICE 1:   Eat in or carry out at the Dogomat, *Delaware's* (emphasis) do-it-yourself dog wash on Route 1. 555-7721.

VOICE 2:   Triple-five, double-seven, two-one.

VOICE 1 (now on board):   Triple-five, double-seven, two-one.

YELLOW PAGES

When you sign up for your business telephone line you get a free listing in the Yellow Pages. Do you need more than that?

You have your choice of categories under which to be listed but the only one that makes sense is "Pet Grooming." Chances are, yours will be the only self-service dog wash among a page of full-service groomers. You have to figure out: how many people interested in full-service grooming are going to turn to the Yellow Pages, see my ad, and decide to wash their dog themselves?

If you conclude there is the potential for significant business from people looking for full-service grooming, you have several options:

◆ **Pump up your listing.** You can pay extra to get your name in all capital letters. Or you can have your listing in boldface or even red instead of black.

◆ **Space Ads.** This is a small bordered ad which stands out in the alphabetical listing. The box containing your name, address and even a logo ranges in size from one-half inch to two inches.

◆ **Display Ads.** These ads can range in size from one column inch to a full page. Check the display ads in your local phone book to see how aggressive the groomers are about chasing business in your trading area. Unless you feel you can win a head-to-head battle with these folks for business, there is no real advantage in spending for a display ad. Research has shown that three out of four shoppers who look something up in the Yellow Pages will make a call and 50% of those will end up with a more attractive ad.

The advantage to Yellow Page advertising is that every household or business has one. The disadvantage is that people are not going to look in the Yellow Pages for a dog wash unless the concept is established in your community. They *will* look you up after they learn of your business from your other promotions to get your number. How big do you want your listing when they come looking specifically for you?

DIRECT MAIL

A response rate of 3% in the direct response business is often considered a success. That means that if you send out 100 letters and get 3 orders you are doing well. If you send out 100 letters, it will cost you $32.00. If you charge $10 for a dog wash and get three customers you make $30. You lose $2 - and that doesn't include the cost of the envelope or printing the flyer or brochure inside. A dog wash is simply not a high enough ticket item to make direct mail pay.

Unless you team up to do a co-operative mailing with other non-competing dog businesses. If you do pull together such a mailing you can obtain a list of dog owners in your trading area from dog magazines who rent their subscription lists. These names are available by zip code and you will need to order a minimum of 5000 at the cost of about $70 per thousand names. The names can be printed on pressure-sensitive labels.

Now let's look at the cost, assuming you and four other businesses will each stuff a flyer into a letter to 5000 dog owners in your area.

5000 envelopes	$35	your share: $7
5000 two-sided flyers	$250	your share: $250
5000 3rd class stamps	$1150	your share: $230
5000 names of dog owners	$350	your share: $70
Total		your share: $557

Assuming a 3% response rate, you can expect 150 new customers. At $10 each that is $1500. Clearly, now direct mail becomes profitable. But you won't be able to do it alone.

If you decide to put together a direct mailing to dog owners in your trading area, spend time considering the envelope - if your envelope doesn't convince the reader to go inside, your mailing is a failure. Here are some tips from the pros:

- ◆ A brightly colored envelope grabs attention.
- ◆ Oversized addressing stimulates the unconscious pleasure people get from seeing their name in print.
- ◆ Use real stamps.
- ◆ Instead of one 34¢ stamp how about using a ten, four fives and one four? Wouldn't you open a letter that someone went to all that trouble to stamp?
- ◆ Use a "teaser" on the envelope to draw people inside: "free offer inside," "big news for dog owners," "what every dog should know."

Another type of direct mail is the coupon mailer or card deck. Being co-operative mailings, these are lower cost alternatives to your own mailings but in all probability still too expensive to support a low-cost, specialty business like a dog wash. And these will be sent to every home in a specific area, half of which will not have a dog in the house so you will be wasting one-half of your advertising dollar immediately.

INTERNET

Setting up a web page and going on the Internet is only an exercise in vanity at this point. The cost of designing a web site (as much as seveal hundred dollars), establishing the site online (about $70) and keeping it running (about $20 a month) is very difficult to recoup in dog washes.

On the positive side, a web page really gives you a chance to tell your whole story to prospects. They will find their way to your web page through your printed material and your advertising. You can even post a sign on the outside of your shop with your web address so busy passers-by can check you out when they arrive home.

Like all costly advertising, if you can team up, it becomes profitable. Find other dog-related businesses to share the cost of the Internet and you can build a site worth visiting. Some of the dog-friendly things your site can include:

- Coupons for services
- Maps and locations of parks in your area which welcome dogs
- A list of hotels in your area which welcome dogs
- A list of apartments which rent to dog owners and their policies
- Calendar of special events
- Puppy of the month pictures
- Reviews of movies with dogs
- A "What's My Mutt?" column for owners of "Heinz 57" dogs to help identify the ancestry of their pet by listing breed characteristics
- Links to dog sites across the Internet universe

OTHER ADVERTISING

There seem to be as many places to advertise your business as there are creative people in the world. You will find out about them as soon as you open your doors for business. Among them:

- **Grocery store register tapes.** Local businesses print their ad on the reverse side of a grocery register tape. Call a business you find on the back of your tape and try to find out a response rate. But half the people who see your ad on the back of a tape won't own a dog.

- **Advertising specialties.** Your dog wash name can be printed on just about anything: pens, post-it pads, shoelaces, dog biscuits.

- **Transport advertising.** Placards can be placed in buses or in bus stop wind shelters.

- **Program advertising.** These can include church programs, charity affairs, school plays, sports team programs. This advertising is not so much to get business as it is to show support for the organization.

Or, you can ignore this entire advertising jungle and just do what we do: strap a sign to your dog that says: I WAS WASHED AT THE DOGOMAT and let her loose in the park.

Starting And Running A Do-It-Yourself Dogwash

Section Three:
Dog Wash-Specific Forms

Running A Do-It-Yourself Dog Wash
Section Three: Dog Wash Specific Forms

1. Cash Flow Variance Report
2. Comment Card
3. Customer Questionnaire
4   Customer Release Form
5. Demographic Matrix
6. Emergency Report
7. Employee Application Form
8. Employee Confidentiality Agreement
9. Employee Personal Data Form
10. Employment Questionnaire
11. Frequent Bather's Club Application
12. Guest Book Sheets
13. Income Variance Report
14. Introductory Period Agreement
15. Job Description Form
16. Manager's Daily Summary Report
17. Manager's Job Agreement
18. Monthly Demographic Totals
19. Pet Sitter Record
20. Supplies Control Log
21. Tip Sheets
    - Car Travel With Your Dog
    - Chocolate Is Poison!
    - Home Pet Clipping
    - How To Clip Toenails
    - How To Pet A Dog
    - Proper Brushing
    - The Perfect Dog Bath
    - Your Dog and Summer
    - Your Dog and Winter
22. Vendor Data Sheet
23. Weekly Money In/Out

Tell us how
we're doing...

_____

_____

_____

_____

_____

_____

_____

_____

_____

We have already been featured in several news stories and expect further media coverage. Is it OK to distribute your comments and/or offer your name to the media to contact for their stories? ❑ Yes ❑ No Thank you for your help.

Tell us how
we're doing...

_____

_____

_____

_____

_____

_____

_____

_____

_____

We have already been featured in several news stories and expect further media coverage. Is it OK to distribute your comments and/or offer your name to the media to contact for their stories? ❑ Yes ❑ No Thank you for your help.

Tell us how
we're doing...

_____

_____

_____

_____

_____

_____

_____

_____

_____

We have already been featured in several news stories and expect further media coverage. Is it OK to distribute your comments and/or offer your name to the media to contact for their stories? ❑ Yes ❑ No Thank you for your help.

Tell us how
we're doing...

_____

_____

_____

_____

_____

_____

_____

_____

_____

We have already been featured in several news stories and expect further media coverage. Is it OK to distribute your comments and/or offer your name to the media to contact for their stories? ❑ Yes ❑ No Thank you for your help.

CUSTOMER SERVICE QUESTIONNAIRE

We are committed to providing you with the finest in pet care service. You can help us by letting us know how we are doing.

Please complete the information below and return the questionnaire at your convenience. Your completed survey will enter you in a monthly drawing for a FREE dogwash. Thank you.

Please check the appropriate boxes.	VERY GOOD	GOOD	AVERAGE	LOUSY
Courtesty and Helpfulness..............	☐	☐	☐	☐
Service Information.........................	☐	☐	☐	☐
Cleanliness....................................	☐	☐	☐	☐
Equipment Quality..........................	☐	☐	☐	☐
Your Overall Dogomat Experience.	☐	☐	☐	☐

We value your input regarding the following questions:

1. Are you aware of our **DOGOMAT** Preferred Customer Club and its benefits to members?

2. Are our times of operation convenient for you? If not what other days/hours do you desire?

3. What pet products would you like to be available for purchase at the **DOGOMAT**?

4. What do you like most about the **DOGOMAT**?

5. What can we do better at the **DOGOMAT**?

6. Are there pet care services which you desire and we do not offer?

7. Comments:

Name:

Address:

CUSTOMER BATHING ASSISTANCE

To be used if Customer desires assistance in bathing dog:

(The cost for this service is $19 per dog)

RELEASE AND HOLD HARMLESS AGREEMENT

The undersigned for and in consideration of the bathing and/or grooming assistance of **THE DOGOMAT** agrees to save and hold harmless **THE DOGOMAT** and its owners, operators, employees, officers and directors from any damage, loss or claims arising from any pre-existing condition of the undersign's pet, either known or unknown to **THE DOGOMAT**.

In the event an emergency should occur with my pet, or in the event special services or handling are required as deemed necessary by **THE DOGOMAT** in the care of my pet, I agree to pay all such costs.

Said damage, loss or claim shall include, but not be limited to, death, injury or shock. Said pre-existing conditions shall include, but not be limited to, advanced age, extreme nervousness, neurosis, illness, malformation or previous injury.

Dated: Pet Owner:

_____   _____

Description of Pet: Address/Phone:

_____   _____

_____   _____

_____   _____

DAILY CUSTOMER DEMOGRAPHIC MATRIX

Manager _____ Date _____ Weather _____

Hours	Customer	Customer	Customer	Customer	Customer	Customer
9-10	M F A B H W 25 40 55 S M L $$$ -	M F A B H W 25 40 55 S M L $$$ -	M F A B H W 25 40 55 S M L $$$ -	M F A B H W 25 40 55 S M L $$$ -	M F A B H W 25 40 55 S M L $$$ -	M F A B H W 25 40 55 S M L $$$ -
10-11	M F A B H W 25 40 55 S M L $$$ -	M F A B H W 25 40 55 S M L $$$ -	M F A B H W 25 40 55 S M L $$$ -	M F A B H W 25 40 55 S M L $$$ -	M F A B H W 25 40 55 S M L $$$ -	M F A B H W 25 40 55 S M L $$$ -
11-12	M F A B H W 25 40 55 S M L $$$ -	M F A B H W 25 40 55 S M L $$$ -	M F A B H W 25 40 55 S M L $$$ -	M F A B H W 25 40 55 S M L $$$ -	M F A B H W 25 40 55 S M L $$$ -	M F A B H W 25 40 55 S M L $$$ -
12-1	M F A B H W 25 40 55 S M L $$$ -	M F A B H W 25 40 55 S M L $$$ -	M F A B H W 25 40 55 S M L $$$ -	M F A B H W 25 40 55 S M L $$$ -	M F A B H W 25 40 55 S M L $$$ -	M F A B H W 25 40 55 S M L $$$ -
1-2	M F A B H W 25 40 55 S M L $$$ -	M F A B H W 25 40 55 S M L $$$ -	M F A B H W 25 40 55 S M L $$$ -	M F A B H W 25 40 55 S M L $$$ -	M F A B H W 25 40 55 S M L $$$ -	M F A B H W 25 40 55 S M L $$$ -
2-3	M F A B H W 25 40 55 S M L $$$ -	M F A B H W 25 40 55 S M L $$$ -	M F A B H W 25 40 55 S M L $$$ -	M F A B H W 25 40 55 S M L $$$ -	M F A B H W 25 40 55 S M L $$$ -	M F A B H W 25 40 55 S M L $$$ -
3-4	M F A B H W 25 40 55 S M L $$$ -	M F A B H W 25 40 55 S M L $$$ -	M F A B H W 25 40 55 S M L $$$ -	M F A B H W 25 40 55 S M L $$$ -	M F A B H W 25 40 55 S M L $$$ -	M F A B H W 25 40 55 S M L $$$ -
4-5	M F A B H W 25 40 55 S M L $$$ -	M F A B H W 25 40 55 S M L $$$ -	M F A B H W 25 40 55 S M L $$$ -	M F A B H W 25 40 55 S M L $$$ -	M F A B H W 25 40 55 S M L $$$ -	M F A B H W 25 40 55 S M L $$$ -
5-6	M F A B H W 25 40 55 S M L $$$ -	M F A B H W 25 40 55 S M L $$$ -	M F A B H W 25 40 55 S M L $$$ -	M F A B H W 25 40 55 S M L $$$ -	M F A B H W 25 40 55 S M L $$$ -	M F A B H W 25 40 55 S M L $$$ -
6-7	M F A B H W 25 40 55 S M L $$$ -	M F A B H W 25 40 55 S M L $$$ -	M F A B H W 25 40 55 S M L $$$ -	M F A B H W 25 40 55 S M L $$$ -	M F A B H W 25 40 55 S M L $$$ -	M F A B H W 25 40 55 S M L $$$ -
7-8	M F A B H W 25 40 55 S M L $$$ -	M F A B H W 25 40 55 S M L $$$ -	M F A B H W 25 40 55 S M L $$$ -	M F A B H W 25 40 55 S M L $$$ -	M F A B H W 25 40 55 S M L $$$ -	M F A B H W 25 40 55 S M L $$$ -

1. Gender   2. Race   3. Age _   4. Dog Size   5. Retail Sales

EMERGENCY REPORT

Date of Emergency _____

Location _____

Description _____
_____
_____
_____
_____

Persons Involved
(address and phone) _____
_____
_____

Pets Involved
(owner name) _____
_____

Employees Present _____
_____

Witnesses
(name, address, phone) _____
_____
_____
_____
_____

Emergency Transport
Physician/Hospital
Veterianarian
Police/Fire Officials _____
_____
_____
_____

Treatment Required _____
_____

Insurance Contact
(name/date/time) _____
_____
_____

Attorney Contact
(name/date/time) _____
_____
_____

Follow-up Action _____
_____
_____

Manager Notes _____
_____
_____
_____
_____
_____

EMPLOYEE APPLICATION FORM

PLEASE PRINT

Name _____ Social Security No. _____

Street Address _____ Apt. no. _____

City _____ State _____ Zip _____

Telephone Number (_____) _____ Date of Birth ____/____/____

How did you hear of job? _____

School Most Recently Attended:

Name _____ City/State _____

Graduated? Yes _____ No _____   Now Enrolled? Yes _____ No _____   Last Grade _____

Three Most Recent Jobs:

1. Company _____ City/State _____

Job Title/Duties _____

Supervisor _____ Phone _____

Dates Worked: from _____ to _____ Salary _____

Reason For Leaving _____

2. Company _____ City/State _____

Job Title/Duties _____

Supervisor _____ Phone _____

Dates Worked: from _____ to _____ Salary _____

Reason For Leaving _____

3. Company _____ City/State _____

Job Title/Duties _____

Supervisor _____ Phone _____

Dates Worked: from _____ to _____ Salary _____

Reason For Leaving _____

U.S. Military

Branch of Service _____ Date Entered _____ Highest Rank _____

Describe service-related skills and experience applicable to civilian employment _____

_____

Physical and Legal

Any health problems or physical defects which could affect your employment? Yes _____ No _____

If so, please explain _____

During the past 10 years have you ever been convicted of a crime, excluding misdemeanors and traffic

violations? Yes _____ No _____ If yes, describe in full _____

_____

Personal References (other than family)

Name _____ Phone _____

Name _____ Phone _____

Name _____ Phone _____

Interviewer or reference comments _____

_____

_____

This Section To Be Filled Out Only After Hire:

Job Title _____ Hourly Rate _____ Start Date _____/_____/_____

Tax Status _____ No. of exemptions _____

Person to contact in case of emergency _____

Phone number _____

---

1. I certify that the information contained in this application is correct to the best of my knowledge and understand that deliberate falsifiaction of this information is grounds for dismissal.
2. I authorize the references listed above to give you any and all information concerning my previous employment and pertinent information they may have, personal or otherwise, and release all parties from all liability for any damage that may result from furnishing same to you.
3. I acknowledge that if I become employed, I will be free to resign at any time for any reason, and that management similarly retains the right to terminate my employment at will.

Signature _____ Date _____

EMPLOYEE CONFIDENTIALITY AGREEMENT

In consideration of my admission to and employment on the premises of _____, hereinafter referred to as the "shop," which I acknowledge is for my benefit, I agree to hold in strict confidence, any proprietary or confidential information which is disclosed or otherwise made available to me, or to which I otherwise gain access, or of which I otherwise obtain knowledge, during or in connection with any visit by me or employment of me on the premises of the shop.

I further agree that I will, during the course of my visit and or employment, whether before, on or after the date hereof:

(a) preserve the privacy of the oral, taped, diagrammed or written information, instructions and or discussions of the shop, its employees, managers, owners, patrons, and vendors.

(b) protect the confidential information used in the shop.

(c) limit disclosure of information to persons outside the shop in relation to known information, techniques, formulas, processes, procedures, plans, designs, statistics and other data.

(d) refrain from soliciting or disrupting shop employees, managers, owners, patrons, or vendors.

I further agree that I have no present intention to use shop procedures, information, materials or equipment for my personal benefit, during or after shop hours, other than that of furthering or implementing the business relationship between the parties to this agreement.

I further agree that I will not remove from the shop premises, nor will I copy or reproduce, any document, material equipment, data or other information of any kind, regardless of form, without the specific permission of the owner of _____.

I further agree that upon termination of my employment, I will return to the shop any and all keys, equipment, documents, materials of any kind including copies, replicas, reproductions and samples.

Dated this _____ day of _____, 19_____ at the address of

_____

in the city of _____, state of _____.

Signature: Witnessed by:

_____   _____

EMPLOYEE PERSONAL DATA SHEET

Name _____ Date of Birth _____

Address _____

_____

Telephone Number _____ Years There _____

Marital Status _____ Name of Spouse _____ Dependents _____

EDUCATION

	Name and City/State	Grade Completed Diplomas/Degrees
College		
High School		
Other		

Military Service _____ Years _____

Highest Rank Obtained _____

Relevant Training/Special Skill _____

_____

WORK EXPERIENCE

Business and City/State	Job Title/Duties	Supervisor	Dates

Trade, professional or civic membership and activities _____

_____

_____

Hobbies, interests, other relevant information _____

_____

_____

Emergency Contact Information _____

_____

EMPLOYMENT QUESTIONNAIRE

Applicant's Name _____ Date _____

Please answer the following questions:

1. Describe your past experience with animals and/or pet grooming.

2. Do you fear animals?

3. Do you have any pet-related allergies?

4. What is the date of your last tetanus booster injection?

5. Do you have arthritis or similar conditions? Do you have back, elbow, or wrist problems?

6. Are you a member of pet-related organizations? If so, which?

FREQUENT BATHER'S CLUB APPLICATION

Membership provides these benefits:

- ◆ *free* subscription to our newsletter
- ◆ *10% off all dog treats and supplies*
- ◆ *your **6th** visit is **free***
- ◆ *invitations to special events*

Owner Name _____

Street _____ Apt _____

City _____ State _____ Zip _____

Home Phone _____

PET NAME _____	PET NAME _____
BREED _____	BREED _____
COLOR _____	COLOR _____
SIZE _____	SIZE _____
BIRTHDATE _____	BIRTHDATE _____
FAVORITE TREAT _____	FAVORITE TREAT _____
❑ MALE ❑ FEMALE	❑ MALE ❑ FEMALE

VISITATION RECORD

Date	Description	Date	Description

Thank You For Visiting Us
Please sign our Guest Book

Date	Name/Pet's Name	Address	Comments

- - -

INCOME STATEMENT VARIANCE REPORT

From the Income Statement Projection For the Month of _____

	A Actual for Month	B Budget for Month	C Deviation (B-A)	D % Deviation (C/B x 100)
Sales				
Less Cost of Goods				
Gross Profit on Sales				

OPERATING EXPENSES
Variable Expenses
      Sales Salaries
      Advertising
      Miscellaneous				

Total Variable Expenses				

Fixed Expenses
      Utilities
      Salaries
      Payroll Taxes/Benefits
      Office Supplies
      Insurance
      Maintenance/Cleaning
      Legal/Accounting
      Delivery
      Licenses
      Boxes, Paper, etc.
      Telephone
      Miscellaneous
      Depreciation
      Interest				

Total Fixed Expenses				
Total Operating Expenses				
Net Profit (Gross Profit on Sales less Total Operating Expenses)				
Tax Expense				
Net Profit After Taxes				

INTRODUCTORY PERIOD AGREEMENT

This letter outlines your Manager Agreement with _____ in which you are asked to accept certain conditions of employment in exchange for a position as Manager with a compensation arrangement that we think you will find reasonable and satisfying. The individual points of the agreement are listed below. Your introductory period is ninety days from date of hire. Satisfactory completion of this introductory period will determine your becoming a regular staff member.

1. During the ninety day period introductory period, you will be paid $_____ monthly salary.

2. At the completion of the introductory period, an evaluation of your performance will be conducted and if employment continues you will be paid $_____ monthly salary.

3. During the introductory period paid sick leave is not available, however, if employment continues after the introductory period you are given _____ paid sick-leave days on a yearly basis (non-accruable). After six months employment, you will be given _____ working days vacation.

4. During the introductory period a review of your progress will take place every thirty days during the introductory period. Thereafter, regular job performance evaluations are given twice annually.

5. You agree that in the event of intentional or willful disregard by you of any projects or employee policies and procedures of _____, the owner shall have the right to take disciplinary action up to and including termination based upon the circumstances of the individual event.

6. The owner will be responsible for your training during the introductory period. The owner will be available for any questions concerning the conditions of your employment and work performance. You may request an interview in writing with the owner.

7. In the event your job performance is not acceptable (below minimum satisfactory levels) employment will not continue.

8. This agreement may be terminated at any time by yourself or _____ during the introductory period. When the introductory period is satisfactorily completed you will become a regular staff member. You will be required to sign a job agreement at the end of the introductory period when employment continues.

Please indicate your acceptance of the above agreement by signing and dating it below. A signed copy of this agreement remains with _____ and a copy is provided for you.

_____   _____
Signature   Date

JOB DESCRIPTION FORM

Position _____

Date Prepared _____

By _____

Task/Function	Estimated Hours Per Week
1.	
2.	
3.	
4.	
5.	
6.	
7.	
8.	
9.	
10.	
Total Hours	

Comments:

Job Description

Job Specifications

MANAGER'S DAILY SUMMARY REPORT

Date _____ Day of Week _____ Hours of Operation _____ Manager _____

PART ONE - CASH RECEIPTS AND BANK DEPOSIT RECORD   Opening Till _____   Next Till _____

CASH RECEIPTS	CASH PAID OUT	CASH REGISTER
Baths........................... _____	Bath Supplies.................. _____	Currency.......................... _____
Rinses/Dips............... _____	Cleaning Supplies........... _____	Coin................................. _____
Grooming.................... _____	Office Supplies............... _____	Checks............................. _____
Shop Sales................. _____	Repairs & Maintenance.... _____	Credit Cards..................... _____
Other.......................... _____	Other.............................. _____	Other............................... _____
Total............ _____	Total................ _____	Total................ _____

BALANCE (Total #1 is equal to Total #2 when in balance)

Total Cash Receipts.. _____   Total Cash Register....................................... _____

Less Total Cash Paid Out............................. _____   Less Opening Till............................ _____

Total #1................................. _____   Total #2..................................... _____

(Enclose cash register tape, sales and cash expense receipts)   **CASH: OVER** _____   **SHORT** _____

BANK DEPOSIT

Total Cash Register................................. _____

Less Next Till.. _____

Total Bank Deposit...................... _____

(Enclose deposit receipts)

Daily Notes:

PART TWO - CASH EXPENSE DETAIL   Total Cash Paid Out _____

Grooming Supplies:

Shampoo/Conditioner.................. _____

Dip/Rinse................................. _____

Towels..................................... _____

Ear Cleaning............................. _____

Other....................................... _____

Building & Equipment Supplies:

Furniture/Fixtures...................... _____

Hardware.................................. _____

Other....................................... _____

Office Supplies:

Postage.. _____

Printed Matter.............................. _____

First Aid....................................... _____

Refreshments............................... _____

Other.. _____

Cleaning Supplies:

Disinfectant/Cleaner..................... _____

Paper Goods................................ _____

Other.. _____

PART THREE - RETAIL SALES DETAIL   Total Pet Products Sold _____

	PET PRODUCTS SOLD	PRICE	QNTY	TOTAL		PET PRODUCTS SOLD	PRICE	QNTY	TOTAL
1.					6.				
2.					7.				
3.					8.				
4.					9.				
5.					10.				

JOB AGREEMENT - MANAGER

This letter outlines your employment agreement with _____ in which you are asked to accept certain condiitons of employment in exchange for the position as Manager together with a compensation arrangement.

1. Under your supervision, _____ is expected to be operated within the standards laid out in the *Operations Manual*.

2. Your management performance of _____ personnel, client and pet care services, safety program, marketing program, records, payroll, employee training, cash receipts, professional working relationships, maintenance, and the achievement of financial and service goals will be formally evaluated twice annually.

3. Your monthly salary of _____ will be paid on the 1st and 15th of every month.

4. Group health insurance is provided effective _____ .

5. You are provided _____ paid sick days per calendar year (non-accruable).

6. After six months employment you are given _____ days paid vacation. You will be given _____ days paid vacation after the second year's employment.

7. The owner is available for questions concerning the conditions of your employment and work performance.

8. You agree that in the event of intentional or willful disregard by you of any projects or employee policies and procedures of _____, the owner shall have the right to take disciplinary action up to and including termination based upon the circumstances of the individual event.

Please indicate your acceptance of the above agreement by signing and dating it below. A signed copy of this agreement remains with _____ owner and a copy is provided for you.

_____   _____

Signature   Date

MONTHLY DEMOGRAPHIC TOTALS

Month/Year _____

Day of the Week

Monday   _____

Tuesday   _____

Wednesday   _____

Thursday   _____

Friday   _____

Saturday   _____

Sunday   _____

Average Retail Sale

_____

Age/Gender Matrix

	25	40	55
Male			
Female			

Gender

Male   _____

Female   _____

Race

Asian   _____

Black   _____

Hispanic   _____

White   _____

Age

Around 25   _____

Around 40   _____

Around 55   _____

Size of Dog

Small Dog   _____

Medium Dog   _____

Large Dog   _____

Hour of the Day (Weekday)

9-10   _____

10-11   _____

11-12   _____

12-1   _____

1-2   _____

2-3   _____

3-4   _____

4-5   _____

5-6   _____

6-7   _____

7-8   _____

Hour of the Day (Weekend)

9-10   _____

10-11   _____

11-12   _____

12-1   _____

1-2   _____

2-3   _____

3-4   _____

4-5   _____

5-6   _____

6-7   _____

7-8   _____

PET SITTER'S INFORMATION RECORD

Courtesy of _____

PET OWNER INFORMATION

Pet Owner

Name _____   Home Phone _____

Street _____   Work Phone _____

City _____   Auto License # _____

State _____ Zip _____   Driver's License # _____

Departure _____
                  (Date and Time)

When my pet is in your care, I can be reached at:

Date _____ Place _____   Telephone _____

Date _____ Place _____   Telephone _____

Date _____ Place _____   Telephone _____

MY PET'S INFORMATION

To assist you in caring for my pet (s), please review the following:

Pet Name 1: _____   Pet Name 2: _____

Breed _____ Color _____   Breed _____ Color _____

Weight _____ M/F _____   Weight _____ M/F _____

Birthdate _____ Age _____   Birthdate _____ Age _____

License # _____   License # _____

(Yes/No) #1 Spayed _____ Collar _____   Tag _____ Leash _____

        #2 Spayed _____ Collar _____   Tag _____ Leash _____

Veterinarian _____   Clinic _____

Street _____   Telephone _____

City _____   Emergency # _____

Please be aware of my pet(s) special medical needs described below:

_____

_____

In an emergency, please take my pet(s) to the nearest animal care facility or to: _____

The name of the person with financial responsibility for my pet during an emergency is:

Name _____   Relationship _____

Street _____   Telephone #1 _____

City _____ State _____ Zip _____   Telephone #2 _____

_____ has an appointment on _____
            (pet)   (Date)

at _____
      (Pet Grooming Salon)   (Address)   (Phone)

SPECIAL INFO

Nutrition _____

Meal Hours _____

My pet likes _____

My pet doesn't like _____

Snacks Okay _____

DO NOT FEED _____

_____   _____
        Signature   Date

SUPPLIES CONTROL LOG

Product _____ Supplier _____ Reorder Level _____

DATE	DESCRIPTION	PURCHASES	USED	BALANCE

Tip Sheet

Car Travel With Your Dog

- When traveling by car, be sure to keep your dog comfortable. Bring alone a favorite toy to make your dog feel secure.

- Do not let your dog stick its head out of the window - this may lead to eye or ear injuries. And do not let your dog travel in the back of an open pickup truck.

- To help your dog overcome motion sickness, take several short trips in the car before your journey. Also, feed your dog lightly before the trip, about one-third the normal amount.

- Make sure your dog has a sturdy leash and collar. The collar should have identification tags, a license, and proof of rabies shots. Your home phone number should be on the tags as well.

- You may want to consider a permanent form of ID - such as a microchip - which can increase the likelihood of reuniting you with your dog if he gets lost far from home.

- Have recent pictures of your dog with you. If you are accidentally separated, these pictures will help local authorities find your dog.

- Take the phone number of your veterinarian and any special medication your dog needs. Some dogs can't adjust to abrupt changes in diet, so pack your dog's regular food, bowls, and a cooler of water.

- If you think you might need to board your dog at some point during your travels, be sure to bring your dog's complete shot records.

- Do not leave your dog unattended. Many dogs bark or destroy property in a strange place.

- Prevent any possibility of unwanted messes. You may want to keep your dog in its crate at night. Also, ask where you should walk your dog when staying at a hotel.

Tip Sheet

Chocolate is Poison!

- For a 50-pound dog a toxic dose of milk chocolate is 50 ounces.

- For a 50-pound dog a toxic dose of semi-sweet chocolate is 15 ounces.

- For a 50-pound dog a toxic dose of baking chocolate is 5 ounces.

- Obviously the chocolate in milk chocolate is diluted and this is why many dogs can eat a piece of chocolate and seem not to show any toxic effects. The problem with feeding a dog milk chocolate treats is that it develops a liking for chocolate. Since dogs do not seem to be as sensitive to bitter tastes as humans it may then eat the more concentrated - and very toxic - baker's chocolate if it gets a chance.

- Treatment is best administered by someone with medical training and follows the same strategy as treatment for caffine overdose:

  * Support Respiration
  * Support cardiovascular function, control arrhythmias, control electrolytes and acid-base   balance
  * Control CNS excitation
  * Emesis
  * Gastric lavage
  * Cathartic
  * Activated charcoal

- (This information can be found in Kirk and Bistner's Handbook of Veterinary Procedures and Emergency Treatment - 6th edition)

Tip Sheet

Home Pet Clipping

- Different clippers are designed to clip different types of hair-coats. Heavily coated breeds or dogs whose coat is matted or heavily tangled require stronger, better quality clippers than light coated breeds.

- The faster a blade moves, the easier and faster it will cut. Better quality clippers have faster motors.

- How fast a blade moves is dictated by the quality and strength of the motor in the clippers as well as how well you lubricate the blade while you clip. **Nyoil** lubricates your blade as you clip to keep its movement free and unimpeded.

- When a blade is moving, friction creates heat which makes the blade hot. Test the blade against your cheek or the inside of your forearm (like a baby bottle) to be sure it isn't uncomfortably hot for your pet. **Nyoil** keeps your blade cool.

- Different blades leave different lengths of hair. The lower the blade number, the longer the hair: a #4F blade leaves 5/8" of hair, a #10 leaves only 1/16" of hair. The #10 is used for smooth or summer cuts, the #4 in winter or for "fuzzy" cuts.

- Smooth faces, feet, the pads of the feet, groin and tummy areas can usually be clipped very close with a #10, #15, or lightly with a #30 or #40 blade to clean them of hair.

- Never clip a dirty dog. Dirt and products such as flea powders destroy the cutting surface of your blade.

- Never clip a wet dog. It's too hard to get through the coat.

- Clipping AGAINST the hair growth pattern leaves shorter hair than clipping WITH the hair growth.

- Store your blade clean, coated with **Nyoil**, wrapped in a paper towel and enclosed in a plastic, air-tight baggie to prevent corrosion from humidity on the cutting surfaces.

Tip Sheet

How To Clip Toenails

- Dogs should have their toenails cut every two to three weeks.

- If the toenails do not need to be cut, the dewclaws usually do.

- If a dog is uncomfortable with clipping, use blinders as a dog is not afraid of what he cannot see. **Teach the dog to stand or sit still and offer his paw, clip off a tiny bit each day for a couple of days in a row.**

- Nails should be cut back as far as possible; if only tipped the quick will come out farther after each clipping.

- Tools needed: toenail clipper, file, silver nitrate, paper towel. If the toenial is cut too short and bleeds, quickly wipe with the towel and apply silver nitrate or baking soda.

- Cutting a white toenail is fairly easy for the pink of the quick is easily seen. Cut right to the point where the pink ends.

- Black nails should be started by taking the hook off. A little black circle will appear in the middle of the nail; the rest of the nail will be whitish. Cut off small sections until the black circle covers almost all of the nail.

- File nails in a sweeping stroke with a file made for dogs' toenails.

- **Always clip the toenails before bathing.** Otherwise bleeding will stain the coat and need to be rewashed.

- Include an examination of the dog's feet into a grooming session to make sure there is nothing stuck betwen the pads. Seeds from some grasses can stab into the pad, pebbles can get stuck, chemicals used on lawns can burn, and fungus can cause friction, which leads to licking, which can lead to hot spots and infection.

Tip Sheet

How To Pet A Dog

Tickling tummies slowly and gently works wonders. Never use a rubbing motion; this makes dogs bad-tempered. A gentle tickle with the tips of the fingers is all that is necessary to induce calm in a dog. I hate strangers who go up to dogs with their hands held to the dog's nose, usually palm towards themselves. How does the dog know that the hand doesn't hold something horrid? The palm should always be shown to the dog and should go straight down to between the dog's front legs and tickle gently with a soothing voice to accompany the action. Very often the dog raises its back leg in a scratching movement, it gets so much pleasure from this.

-Barbara Woodhouse

Tip Sheet

Proper Brushing

Short-haired dogs

- Brush in circular motion with curry comb made of rubber with teeth cut into edges. It will pull the dead coat out.

- Slicker brushes will take out the dead undercoat. Start on the legs and hold outer hair so that you can brush from the skin outward. If it is not removed, the coat will easily mat. Use this technique all over the dog - legs / body / tail. Dogs resent the tail being brushed so save it for last.

Fine-haired dogs

- Use a natural-bristle brush.

- Moisten area to be worked with a good coat conditioner.

Long-haired dogs

- Use a pin brush if not tangled; a slicker brush if coat is tangled.

- Start at the legs, brushing from the skin out and brushing only a few hairs at a time. **The secret to thorough brushing is to brush only a few hairs at a time.**

- Check each area with a comb; if the comb goes through without stress continue all the way up to the middle of the dog's back. Go to the loin area and to the back legs; then move to each side of the back of the dog.

Badly matted dogs

- Use a hard slicker brush but scissor coat to desired length first.

- Spray coat with "mats away" and pat cornstarch into the coat with a piece of cotton. Wait ten minutes and then follow the brushing routine.

Tip Sheet

The Perfect Dog Bath

- Improper bathing can cause a matted condition in the coat which is uncomfortable to your dog; completely comb all tangles out of the dog's coat before starting.

- **The right way to bathe a dog is determined by the texture and length of coat**. Short-haired dogs are washed with a vigorous circular motion which will pull out the dirt. On dogs with a medium-length coat, use a back-and-forth motion. As the hair gets longer, go only in the direction the hair grows.

- **Step 1**: Rinse the dog completely.

- **Step 2**: Apply the shampoo along the back, working up as much lather as possible; do the same with the belly, legs and tail.

- **Step 3**: Rinse the coat with one hand to run water on the dog and the other hand in a kneading fashion to work the soap out. **Make certain all the soap is out as dried soap will dull a coat and cause skin problems.**

- **Step 4**: Before towel-drying, squeeze as much water out of the coat as possible by pulling the hair straight out and squeezing at the same time.

- **Step 5**: Use a washcloth to clean the dog's face and avoid getting water in his ears. Moisture inside the ears provides the conditions for fungus infections.

- Dogs with thick coats must be wet to the skin for effective bathing, and the shampoo must be thoroughly rinsed to keep the skin and coat clean and healthy. Before rinsing, try to scrape the lather off using your hand. Check for residue by squeezing the hair; if you see any bubbles, keep rinsing.

- Towel dry every dog and use a hand-held hair dryer on thick-coated dogs. Guard against chills.

- When blowdrying your dog, follow the rule that the longer the hair, the closer you hold the nozzle to the skin. This will prevent tangling. Lay the nozzle parallel to the skin and blow water off the hair from the skin outward.

Tip Sheet

Your Dog And Summer

- Never leave your dog unattended in direct sunlight or in a closed vehicle. Heatstroke can occur and lead to brain damage or death. Signs of heatstroke are panting, drooling, rapid pulse and fever. Immediately immerse the dog in cool water and seek emergency veterinary assistance.

- If you absolutely must leave your dog in the car, park in the shade, make sure the windows are slightly ajar so he can get air, and leave some fresh water.

- Beware of insect bites. If your dog is bitten or stung, remove the stinger and watch the site for an allergic reaction. If this occurs or there have been multiple wasp, bee or mosquito bites, take the animal to the vet.

- Check your dog daily for fleas and ticks.

- Most lawn and garden products may be hazardous. Make sure that plants and fertilizers within the dog's reach are not toxic.

- The outdoors exposes dogs to the elements. Dogs may need extra brushing and bathing to stay clean and healthy.

- Try to avoid strenuous exercise with your dog on extremely hot days and refrain from physical activity when the sun's heat is most intense.

- Always make sure your dog has access to fresh water.

- Heartworm is a common problem for dogs. Take your dog to a vet for a heartworm check every spring.

Tip Sheet

Your Dog And The Holidays

- The holidays are not ideal for introducing a pet into your family. New puppies and dogs require extra attention and a stable environment, which the holiday season often doesn't permit. A puppy is not a toy that can be returned. Experts suggest giving a festively wrapped can of dog food or a leash as a symbol of the dog to come.

- Holly, mistletoe and poinsettia plants are pet poisons! Make sure they are kept in places your dog cannot reach.

- Remove holdiay lights from lower tree branches. They may get very hot and burn dogs.

- Beware of electrical cords which pets often try to chew. Places wires out of reach.

- Refrain from using edible ornaments. Your dog may knock the tree over in an attempt to eat them.

- Whether your tree is live or artificial, both kinds of needles are sharp and indigestible. Keep your tree fenced in or in a room that can be blocked off.

- Tinsel is dangerous for dogs. It may obstruct circulation and, if swallowed, block the intestines.

- Alcohol and chocolate are toxic for dogs, even in small amounts. Keep eggnog, sweet treats and other seasonal goodies out of reach.

- Avoid using glass ornaments. They break easily an may cut a dog's feet and mouth.

- The holiday season is a stressful time for dogs. Try to keep a normal schedule during all the excitement.

Tip Sheet

Your Dog And Winter

- Don't leave your dog outside in the cold for long periods of time. Be attentive to your dog's body temperature and limit time outdoors.

- Groom your dog regularly. Your dog needs a well-groomed coat to keep him properly insulated. Short- or coarse-haired dogs may get extra cold so consider a sweater or coat. Long-haired dogs should have their paw hair clipped to ease snow removal and the cleaning of their feet.

- Feed your dog additional calories if he spends a lot of time outdoors or is a working animal. It takes more energy in the winter to keep body temperature regulated, so additional calories are necessary.

- Towel or blow-dry your dog if he gets wet from rain or snow. It is important to dry and clean his paws, too. This helps avoid tiny cuts and cracked pads.

- Antifreeze, which often collects on driveways and roadways, is highly poisonous. Although it smells and tastes good to your dog, it can be lethal.

- Rock salt, used to melt ice on sidewalks, may irritate footpads. Be sure to rinse and dry your dog's feet after a walk.

- Frostbite is a winter hazard. To prevent frostbite on ears, tail, and feet, don't leave your dog outdoors for too long. Adequate shelter is a necessity. Keep your dog warm, dry and away from drafts. Tiles and uncarpeted areas may become extremely cold, so make sure to place blankets and pads on floors in these areas.

- Be very careful of supplemental heat sources. Fireplaces and portable heaters can severely burn your dog. Make sure all fireplaces have screens and keep portable heaters out of reach.

- Like people, dogs seem to be more susceptible to illnesses in the winter. Make sure to take your dog to a veterinarian if you see any suspicious symptoms.

Tip Sheet

Your Dog At The Beach

- The majority of dogs can swim and love it, but dogs entering the water for the first time should be tested; never throw your dog into the water. Start in shallow water and call your dog's name - or try to coax him in with a treat or toy. Always keep your dog within reach.

- Another way to introduce your dog to the water is with a dog that already swims and is friendly with your dog. Let your dog follow his friend.

- If your dog begins to doggie paddle with his front legs only, lift his hind legs and help him float. He should quickly catch on and will keep his back end up.

- Swimming is a great form of exercise, but don't let your dog overdo it. He will be using new muscles and may tire quickly.

- Be careful of strong tides that are hazardous for even the best swimmers.

- Cool ocean water is tempting to your dog. Do not allow him to drink too much sea water. Salt in the water will make him sick. Salt and other minerals found in the ocean can damage your dog's coat so regular bathing is essential.

- Check with a lifeguard for daily water conditions - dogs are easy targets for jellyfish and sea lice.

- Dogs can get sunburned, especially short-haired dogs and ones with pink skin and white hair. Limit your dog's exposure when the sun is unusually strong and apply sunblock to his ears and nose 30 minutes before going outside.

- If your dog is out of shape, don't encourage him to run on the sand. Running on the beach is strenuous exercise and a dog that is out of shape can easily pull a tendon or ligament.

- Provide plenty of fresh water and shade for your dog.

VENDOR DATA SHEET

Vendor _____ Contact _____ Phone _____

Address _____ Fax _____

DATE	PRODUCT ORDERED	PURCHASE #	COMMENTS

WEEKLY MONEY IN/OUT   Week of _____

TOTAL MONEY IN

DAY	WASHES		TREATS		SHOP		AMOUNT	
MON								
TUE								
WED								
THUR								
FRI								
SAT								
SUN								
Total This Week								
Total Up To Last Week								
Total To Date								

MILEAGE

MON		
TUE		
WED		
THUR		
FRI		
SAT		
SUN		
TOTAL		

NOTES

PAYROLL

EMPLOYEE	TOTAL WAGES	DEDUCTIONS				NET PAID	
		SOCIAL SECURITY	FEDERAL INC TAX				

EXPENDITURES

ACCT NO.	ACCOUNT	TOTAL THIS WEEK		TOTAL UP TO LAST WEEK		TOTAL TO DATE	
	DEDUCTIBLE						
1	MERCHANDISE/MATERIALS						
2	ACCOUNTING						
3	ADVERTISING						
4	AUTO EXPENSE						
5	CARTONS, ETC.						
6	CONTRIBUTIONS						
7	DELIVERY EXPENSE						
8	ELECTRICITY						
9	ENTERTAINMENT						
10	FREIGHT & EXPRESS						
11	HEAT						
12	INSURANCE						
13	INTEREST						
14	LAUNDRY						
15	LEGAL EXPENSE						
16	LICENSES						
17	MISCELLANEOUS EXPENSE						
18	OFFICE EXPENSE						
19	POSTAGE						
20	RENT						
21	REPAIRS						
22	SHOP EXPENSE						
23	TAX - SOCIAL SECURITY						
24	TAX - STATE UNEMPLOYMENT						
25	TAX - OTHER						
26	SELLING EXPENSE						
27	SUPPLIES						
28	TELEPHONE						
29	TRADE DUES, ETC.						
30	TRAVELING EXPENSE						
31	WAGES & COMMISSION						
32	WATER						
33							
34							
35							
	SUB-TOTAL						
	NON-DEDUCTIBLE						
51	NOTES PAYABLE						
52	FEDERAL INCOME TAX						
53	LOANS PAYABLE						
54	LOANS RECEIVABLE						
55	PERSONAL						
56	FIXED ASSETS						
57							
	TOTAL THIS WEEK						
	TOTAL UP TO LAST WEEK						
	TOTAL TO DATE						

DETAIL OF WEEKLY EXPENDITURES

MERCHANDISE AND MATERIALS PAID BY CASH AND CHECKS						OTHER EXPENDITURES BY CHECK AND CASH					
DAY	TO WHOM PAID	CHECK NO.	ACCT. NO.	AMOUNT		DAY	TO WHOM PAID	CHECK NO.	ACCT. NO.	AMOUNT	
	TOTAL THIS WEEK						TOTAL THIS WEEK				

35591483R10106

Made in the USA
San Bernardino, CA
29 June 2016